A Pleiadian Starseed from Alcyone

Dianne Zimmermann

ISBN 978-1-9957077-58-1

Publishing Assistance
BookCrafters, Parker, Colorado.
www.BookCrafters.net

I dedicate this book to my friends whose never-ending encouragement drove me on when the going got tough.

Acknowledgements

I wish to thank my friends for all their interest and encouragement in all my writing endeavors. I wish to express special thanks to my friends Lou Platten and LA Mott for their years of encouragement, ideas, proofreading, and editing skills.

Chapter One:

A Starseed

Call the contents of this book, far out, call it fiction, call it unbelievable if you wish. Sometimes I find it a bit unbelievable myself; but rather, I have faith in our collective soul energy. And I am very connected with the Pleiadians, so I think what I am writing about is quite magical, and if we believe, may even help save this planet and its human inhabitants. I feel gifted, protected, blessed, and very special. But I believe there are many starseeds from other star systems that are here on Earth at this time too, to help. This is just my story.

I am a star-seed from Alcyone, the central and brightest star of the Pleiades. How do I know that I am a Pleiadian starseed? Well, I have had the blessed and distinct pleasure and privilege of the Pleiadians themselves telling me so. The Pleiadians showed up one evening while I was speaking in a mediumship meeting. I was about to begin to say that I just had this feeling, this knowing, that I was from the Pleiades. But before I could say more they, yes, the Pleiadians themselves, told me so in front of two witnesses. And these two witnesses have my highest regard and respect as they are highly qualified and reputable professional psychic mediums. Needless to say, it was a miraculous moment for all of us.

The year was 2015, I was attending an intuition mediumship class at Mystic Valley Gem and Book Store in St. Louis. Most of the people had already left the room, as there were only the three of us. In retrospect, I think the Pleiadians planned it that way. So it was just for we three to be there in the room when they choose to show up and verify where I was from. I was speaking about the Pleiades from where I always felt and thought I was from. Intuitively I had always resonated with the words Pleiades and Pleiadians, ever since I first heard the words in my early twenties. It just fit. I think my guides had planned it to happen just the way that it did. As I was speaking and about to say where I thought I was from, I was suddenly interrupted by my instructor Julia Marie.

"Do you feel them?" she asked. "They are in the room with us."

"Yes," Linda said, she too was suddenly drawn to the wave of energy in the room as I was. I could feel their energy and even see a wave of energy in my mind's eye.

"I do," I said, and did I ever feel them. Of course they were there on this day just for me, and so their presence just for me would be witnessed.

We all felt their energy in the corner near the table where we three sat. I saw that energy wave flash. It was magical. Then Julia Marie spoke again.

"They said to tell you that you are from A-l-c-y-o-n-e, Alcyone, they even spelled it out for you," Julia Marie said.

"I feel so honored," I said. Linda and I also got the same message as Julia Marie got it. I don't know about the other two, but it was a very magical spiritual moment for me. I felt honored to experience that magical blessed moment and it's one I will never forget. Talk about flying high! I mean how often does that happen, where extraterrestrials beings from another star system come and tell you that is where you are from and tell you that you are a star-seed? So I feel very special that the Pleiadians came to tell me personally that I was a Pleiadian star-seed from Alcyone, the brightest and central star, of the Pleiades. I considered it an honor to be a star-seed from Alcyone of the Pleiades and to be told by them that I am. I had always been very curious about the Pleiadians, ever since I first heard the word, so I have read a lot about the Pleiades star system that is in the Taurus constellation. I now realize the Pleiadians themselves sparked that interest in me.

I also experienced a Pleiadian energy wave and felt them one time on a hike more recently to Boynton Canyon near Sedona, AZ. I was hiking near the top to where people usually gather. A young woman ahead of me already there asked me a question as I neared her.

"Where is the Vortex?" the young woman asked as she stood a few feet before me.

"I always thought it was near the most twisted little

juniper pine trees," I said. And we were near several of the little twisted trees.

"I am seeing like an energy wave," she said. It flashed between her and me, and I saw it too.

"I am seeing an energy wave, too," I said. We both were amazed. I told her it was a sign for her and me that the Pleiadians were there. It was magical. My guides had me tell her more.

"You know most of the Native American Indian tribes say they are from the Pleiades," I told her. It was a magical moment for both of us.

Once before when I sat up there on the big rocks, I saw the spiritual image of a Native American woman. It is indeed a very spiritual area and should be approached with great spiritual reverence. It is sacred ground. The Southwest and Sedona area is home to many tribes: Apache, Hopi, Navaho, and they all believe they came from the Pleiadians as I know now that I do too. The Cherokee from Tennessee and other states also claim to be from the Pleiades.

There are stories from a Hopi granddaughter who tells of visiting her grandfather. When a visiting Pleiadian craft landed in the driveway, and she watched from the kitchen window as her grandfather reacted as if a neighbor pulled up in the yard to visit. She was amazed at how he walked out to them casually and smiling to greet them. The invading evil reptilian terrorist illuminati managed to crush that magical history.

And you don't think evil reptiles are running the show? I can't help but think if women were even considered equal, they would come visit the Americas peacefully, perhaps trade recipes and crafting skills. Get it? Women do not have the evil reptilian humanoid hybrid brain that most white males have. And who, without the moral compass of a soul, have scratched and clawed their way to the top of the heap of evil, dishonestly, greed, dominating corporate and government positions. The Pleiadians have protected me as I have not been taken in by the false flags and clandestine evil that lurks.

Of course, I feel blessed and special as I have been spared the hypocrisy. I have come to feel they must have me on a special mission. On a mission to observe what is going on in the world now and to use modern methods of social platforms to share my experiences. Realize it or not people, these are scary times with evil reptilian plans to exterminate more humans from this planet toward their totalitarian New World Order (NWO), World Health Organization (WHO) regime, soon to come into our reality, if we are not careful. The sneaky living in the ground reptiles, wish to rise up from the depths of hell and claim the Earth as their own. More about that later. There are many of us starseeds here at this time to help humankind.

Perhaps the reason I am a starseed from Alcyone of the Pleiades here on Earth at this time is to help enlighten humans. Starting with telling them to meditate and raise their vibrations into the mystical spiritual fifth dimension of collective soul love. We are in the fifth dimension now, in the age of Aquarius, the age of feminine rule where love will prevail over the evil that rules, and the evil will dissipate and go away.

The reptilian humanoid hybrid males in high corporate and government positions who are slaves for the underground reptiles are losing their power, because the world is beginning to awaken and see their egotistical narcissistic sick, satanic, sexual molesting repertory ways. And I feel the Pleiadians are here to help us humans and just in the nick of time. The Pleiadians are members of the Galactic Federation that is monitoring what is happening on planet Earth now in 2024.

And no better time than now. Because the evil reign needs to stop now according to the evil reptilian humanoid hybrids in power. They have their demonic agenda intended plans of establishing full reptilian rule over humans by 2030. I have read so much about this in the many books written by David Icke, Brad Olsen, Len Kasten, and Elana Freeland. I believe their last evil attack, I hope it is the last, was that of the evil c19fake virus to mandate their toxic jab attack onto the people. Many people were taken in by the propaganda and readily stood in line and rolled up their sleeves, only for many to suffer horrendous on-going side effects. Thankfully, many seem to be fine; but many have suffered horrendous side effects from the ingredients that make up the jabs. For many seemed to have an ill effect on their nervous system causing them to have constant shaking, turbo lung cancers, strokes, blood clots, kidney stones, heart attacks and strange things happening to male and female reproductive systems. I asked my Pleiadian guides to help me understand why what seemed to be an attack on the people was happening.

It is time to try to help heal the people who were injured. Personally I do not see how they can assume that one size fits all when it comes to pills and injections. Every human body is different and many people have preconditions and are already on medicines that perhaps the injections did not coincide or mix with well. Its only common sense! Are we under attack? Have we been manipulated? Yes, according to David Icke and others. There are many books brave souls have written.

David Icke claims we are being programmed by the frequencies coming from the Moon. Yes, he does, and it only gets more interesting. He calls it the hive brain manipulations from the frequencies sent out from the Moon's computer. Interesting concept! I believe the c19 debacle had been planned for years. And the attack on the people was to cause illness and death over time to look like natural appearing deaths.

When I was kid, people never used to be this sick, of course everything was organic, everything! Now, today, it seems as if our whole economy is based on poor health, your poor health. Our modern day main street media pushed, propagandized, commercialized medicine world, our economy is based on poor health across the board. Get it? It is part of the reptile led illuminati elite's depopulation plan that is being geared up. Recently, I heard Dr. Bryan Ardis say on Jonathon

Otto's site, "They can't kill everyone off at once, think about how obvious that would look. Rather like a serpent snake, it is done in a silent, deadly, sneaky matter." This can't possibly be happening, I thought; so, I did some more research.

I know the Pleiadians speak through me through my *DianneTheMedium* podcast on PodBean. I believe the Pleiadians have me, a starseed (Delores Cannon calls us waves of volunteers) on a mission at this crucial time. I believe they gave me the idea in July of 2023 to do a podcast . After I visited Jonathon Otto's site, I was appalled to read by Dr. Bryan Ardis, that snake venom is in the c19 jabs. What? I had to read it twice, as I could not believe what I read. If it's true, it certainly could not have been an accident. Who brings snake venom into a scientific lab unless they planned to use it? It was the only place I saw that information. I know my guides led me to that site to read that and to listen to Dr. Bryan Ardis suggestions on what to do to counter snake venom side effects. Because he said that now they, along with mind dulling toxic fluoride, are adding snake venom to city water supplies. I don't know about you, but that sure does not give me a warm fuzzy feeling about who or what is running this government! Dr. Bryan Ardis said that nicotine could counter the snake venom effect. Here are a few things that contain nicotine that Dr. Bryan Ardis mentioned: Nicotine patch or gum, Melatonin, cabbage, pineapple, potatoes, black peppers, cayenne peppers, and all colorful peppers, plums, and raisins.

Seems to me the poisoning is occurring in many

different ways. One example is the constant daily spraying of chem trails. I mean you can't help but notice those heavy, thick, long, crisscrossed chemtrails that cover the sky and occur on most days. The book, *Geoengineered Transhumanism, How the Environment has been weaponized by chemicals, electromagnetism, and nanotechnology for synthetic biology* by Elana Freeland, says lessens our oxygen supply and slowly suffocates plant and animal life. Plants and trees and sunlight are very important to sustaining life on planet Earth. And chem trails are becoming heavier and thicker and are sprayed globally now. Seems the powers that be, in government and our modern-day medical system, happen to be a forest of untruths. Look at the big picture.

When I was a kid, everything was organic up until the later 1970s when big chemical bought off the government. When I was a kid, I waited for the school bus to come and the springtime air smelled so fresh, the water running in the ditch was clear. There were plants growing, and birds singing. I witnessed tadpoles swimming in the ditch. You will not see that today! Not today, not with big chemical companies spraying and pouring toxic chemicals on everything. In recent years big chemical has come up with genetically modified organisms, that have no nutritional value whatsoever. It is actually toxic to the human system and doctors are into pushing band aids to allow the toxic process to go on. Get the feeling they are trying to bump you off?

All doctors know to do is to hand out various band

aids pills. So, I understand, they themselves along with the public have been brainwashed, mind controlled, just to push surgeries, and shell out pills and jabs, without being the least bit concerned about finding out the root cause of illness. They don't care! Down deep, subconsciously they know the truth is a plan to depopulate humans from the planet by the evil reptiles that lurk underground. And of course, if they would investigate and question, they would learn that all pills are mere band aids that make you feel good while your body's health further deteriorated. In an interview on Conscious Media Network, season one episode one, and season eight, episode five, I heard Dr. Harvey Bigelsen say allopathic medicine has not cured a single illness ever and only contributed to more illnesses. He was kicked out of the American Medical Association (AMA) for actually trying to help people heal. Pretty amazing isn't it.

Instead of modern medicine making our lives healthier, we are seeing horrific and permanent maiming, and negative jab side effects are becoming the norm. I believe the Pleiadians have me here on planet Earth at this time for a reason. Delores Cannon suggests there are at least three waves of volunteers that have come to Earth to help. I am a member of the first wave of volunteers to come to Earth. I am here to witness and try to awaken people to these atrocities humans have been mind controlled to not see. How can it not appear to me that our very own government seems to be in cahoots with big drug and chemical companies?

Actually as I write this, I am a little afraid I might get bumped off, but more and more like-minded people are waking up to the criminal activities (that is, if we had laws to protect the people) and evil atrocities that are happening. Isn't it obvious they have no respect for human life? Look at the wars, the time when evil thugs rise up to attack for dominance, for profits, and excuses to torture, rape, maim and kill. Duh! Evil lurks in high places. Earth needs extraterrestrials help, now! Why do you think that even back in 1952 those space craft encircled the capitol, and then again a year later? They were trying to tell the evil ones, to cool it!

We starseed volunteers have asked our Pleiadian guides and their friends to get the Galactic Federation to run interference on our behalf and help us clean up this unhealthy destructive mess we have come to try to live with. They need to get here soon, because the plan is to have all humans left remaining on Earth to be digitally chipped and programed to the hive mind programming of the computerized Moon. The reptiles have tweeted the Moon's mind controlling computer and made it worse, causing a worse matrix for the humans on Earth to be entrapped in. Humans will lose more and more freedoms, as already the reptilian humanoid hybrids running the show, pretty much know our every move, our habits, and our health issues. Chemical based pills and jabs do not work on humans and are mere band aids. Our immune systems can only thrive on natural organic healthy vitamins and minerals, and they know that.

So if organic foods go away, we too go away, into extinction.

I believe I am a starseed from Alcyone of the Pleiades here for a reason, and that is to use the internet, my DianneTheMedium.com web site, my podcast on *DianneTheMedium* at PodBean, and to write books. I believe the Pleiadians have me on a mission to try to get the word out that perhaps mind to mind we can unite our souls and our heartfelt energies of love to help to overcome the heartless, soulless, evil that seems to lurk everywhere and seems to me to be ramping up and gaining more control of everything. It is sad to have to say this at the beginning of the new year of 2024, as I write this. So meet with your friends, and help get the word out to the Galactic Federation members, that are hovering and circling earth and who wait for us to summon their help. I say Galactic Federation, forget that non-interfering clause and help us humans as we are innocent victims.

My Pleiadian family has members in the Galactic Federation and have helped me prepare for this mission that I believe I am honored to be on. I have been conditioned by the Pleiadians to be drawn to read certain books to learn what I need to know for this mission I am on Earth for during this unique and threatening time in human history. Sure everything appears to be fine; that is, if one is only watching local and national network news. And listening and obeying the medical system and getting your medical wellness visits in, so the MK-Ultra trained robotic minded pill and jab pushers can get their points and commissions accumulated and meet their pharmaceutical master's quotas. My Pleiadian guides led me to observe and believe that big chemical corporations are behind the sickening of humans as they push of toxic weed killer, created genetically modified organisms, corn and soybeans and other foods. So it appears to me that on one hand they are trying to poison us. And on the other hand try to convince us that they are trying to keep us well. Why should we believe them? Why all of a sudden are they so worried about our health so much to mandate a free and untested jab to humans? And why have they passed laws to protect themselves from lawsuits? Duh? According to Dr. Bryan Ardis, there is snake venom in them-there c19 jabs. It's hard to comprehend, isn't it? That your own government would allow this! The snake venom jabs were created in China, using King cobra and Crane cobra snake venoms according to Dr. Bryan Ardis. He says they will now be adding it to city water supplies, along with fluoride. Yes, that fluoride, the waste product of manufacturing aluminum.

I have been directed and led by the Pleiadians to do the research. They lead me to the books, and to view selected programs on Netflix, and GAIA. They guide me to shows they want me to see. We humans need to use our spiritual powers and rise above as love will win over evil. Cathy O'Brien says the same thing. More about her later. I wish to learn more and to help aid and usher humans into the fifth dimension.

Feminine rule is needed. Actually it's much needed

at this time as we are in the fifth dimension of Aquarian feminine rule of love and cooperation. We do not need any more evil reptilian humanoid hybrid patriarchal hate and greed. Maybe if we give them some of their own medicine. You know like addictive black tar heroin-based Xanax, Ativan, Adderall, or Ritalin to dull them down. Humans are better than this, with a loving soul, we all are spiritual beings here on Earth as human beings, when our bodies die, our souls, our spiritual being lives on. So meditate, get into nature, go organic and holistic.

I wish to help elevate humans above all this mess, by having them get out in nature, to meditate, to raise their vibrations and go holistic and organic. I believe my Pleiadian guides have led me to learn all I can about this seemingly failed government oversight to protect unsuspecting people from what appears to be a band aid only run medical system. Get it? If they are purposely making you sick with bad air, water, food, drugs, they are certainly not going to suddenly become benevolent saints and want to help you heal yourself. Besides only we humans can heal ourselves through our own built-in pharmacy, our immune system. And that is the only way! Sure seems to me that propagandized selling of petroleum based pills, untested or poorly tested jabs, and toxic GMO foods are becoming ever more present. In my summation, a deceitful, truth covered-up world of toxic trickery is an act of treason. Where is the law? Where are the courts of law? Where is the oversight, as the government is supposed to be overseeing what corporations try to sell to us? I thought government was our friend. Apparently not! Apparently the evil greedy reptilian humanoid hybrids without soul or consciousness can be bought. Greed and money rule in a reptilian humanoid hybrid world.

May I suggest watching Painkiller on Netflix. Really, watch it, it'll knock your socks off to see the painful truth. I can't help but think that my Pleiadian guides, wanted me to see this atrocity just for what it is. Just where is the law, and the moral decency? What about the Nuremberg trials after WWII? Oh, that was just a show wasn't it, as sixteen hundred highest ranking Nazis were slipped through the Vatican to North and South America to escape trials. But if everyone is in on it, who will initiate those trials on behalf of the humans now?

It appears to me there isn't any law or government officials to protect us. It seems they all have been bought off. And they are all corrupt programmed reptilian humanoid hybrid enslaved males, mere puppets of the Illuminati who are mere underling slaves answering to the evil satanic reptiles living underground. Oh yes! Look at the front cover of *Children of the Matrix* by David Icke. My Pleiadians guides led me to learn this. David Icke is one of us, a Pleiadian. He has his sun in Taurus in his Astrological birth chart. More about that later.

They, the reptilian humanoid hybrid slaves, are doing the bidding of their evil-minded reptile masters who are pulling the toxic strings toward our slow unsuspicious demise. Seems ill health, that is driving us to medical facilities, is what holds up our total economy especially in the last fifty years. Surgery or chemicals are the only treatments. If we were all healthy, then the toxic for-profit allopathic medical industry would make no money. See the conspiracy in it all? At this point petroleum and illness is holding up our economy. And it is part of the plan leading us to the evil destruction of a majority of the populace for the Agenda 2030 Great Reset so desired by the Globalist. Get it? Are you finally catching on?

Don't believe me, do your own research. I can only summarize from what I have witnessed, read and have learned by doing my research on world events and learning about the Pleiadians. It seems to be that maybe human destruction is what the underground reptiles want as they want to roam the surface of Earth. The sun hurts their reptilian eyes. Just one of the reasons to cover it up; I suspect that is why we have daily sprayings of toxic aluminum and barium chemtrails. Aluminum dulls our brains and barium wrecks our immune systems. By the way, aluminum is in statins to curb your high cholesterol, which you really need to keep clear thinking and memory. Get it? I was listening to an interview with Elena Freeland recently. She added two more chemicals to the list, besides aluminum and barium, that are being sprayed on us to dull us down, and to decrease our oxygen supplies. Sorry, I did not recognize or catch those two chemicals, so did not get to take notes. I learned that the oceans help clean the air as trees do and take in carbon monoxide and give off oxygen. So that explains why they cut down forests and destroy vegetation. Get the picture? Trees are our source of oxygen. And all living organisms need the benefits of the sun. Without the sun all living things will perish. Is that the plan? So I try to learn all that I can about what is actually going on, only because our very lives depend on it. Now more about me and the Pleiadians.

My Pleiadian guides have led me to watch the "Galactic Messages" and "Conscious Media Network" series on GAIA and to read books by Barbara Marciniak. I have gone to Raleigh, NC and to Sedona, AZ to attend many of her seminars where she channels the Pleiadians. I feel privileged that they appeared and told me that I am from Alcyone of the Pleiades. I wish to honor that privilege by doing good deeds, by doing research to awaken and enlighten fellow souls to rise above the evil that is obviously lurking everywhere.

The Pleiadians have led me to believe that reptilian humanoid hybrid evil lurks in high places. I have read books by Barbara Hand Clow who is also from Alcyone. I have seen her interviewed by Regina Meredith on Open Minds on GAIA. Barbara Hand Clow says she has her second home there and goes back and forth from Earth to Alcyone on a regular basis while she is in a deep sleep state. I have learned the benevolent Pleiadians are far more advanced than humans on Earth, as greed has held back benevolent technical advances and has kept Earth in the greedy malevolent petroleum Stone Age. All because greedy reptilian humanoid hybrids males are controlled by the Illuminati who answer to the full-blooded reptilians lurking underground. Old time combustion engine auto makers have killed the electric car technology or certainly restricted it and slowed its progress way down. Humans should be embarrassed and irate to be held back, just because there is still oil in the ground. Oil pollution is the problem--not cow farts. But we get false flag propaganda as big chemical wishes to eliminate all animal meats and serve up fake meats - toward our demise. It's an insult to humans' mental, and physical health as it becomes more obvious that they are in the process of eliminating humans from the planet. My research has led me to believe that the original looking reptiles living underground wish to roam on the surface, so they have their trained stooges, the Reptilian humanoid hybrids, mostly white, bastard males of the illuminati families. And they are strategically distributed and positioned around the world in positions as leaders. The Pleiadians are watching and trying to warn us.

The Pleiadians and other star systems use zero-point anti-gravity technology and can operate spacecraft controlled by their thoughts, or they can just travel in spirit from one point to another and appear at their destination without the use of a spacecraft. I believe that is how many come to Earth when summoned by humans. I have written about that in my books, *Just a Thought Away*, and in my book entitled, *Verda*.

I have recently read on Aurora Pleiadian Messages that now at the beginning of the year 2024, as I write this, the Pleiadians and the Galactic Federation have many spacecraft hovering and encircling planet Earth. They are in position and eager to help save planet Earth and all its inhabitants that have souls. Plants, animals, humans have souls. Evil reptilian humanoid hybrid males do not. The Galactic Federation and the Pleiadians are ready for us to summon them to help save planet Earth from the evil satanic underground forces who have ruled Earth for thousands of years. It is too obvious to me and frankly I do not see how any conscious soul-being can deny the poisoning that is going on. Where is the law to protect the people? It appears to me that humans are not in control; satanic worshiping reptilian humanoid hybrids, slaves of the evil satanic Reptiles, are running things.

As evidence, we see the EPA is now allowing even more toxins to be put in city water supplies besides fluoride, and snake venom, according to Dr. Bryan Ardis. We have even more GMO, non-nutritional foods to eat, and chemtrails to cover up the sun, covering our skies and raining down on us. It is so blatant, and they are becoming even more open and obnoxious about it as time goes on. It's like they, the cabal, the globalist suddenly got into high gear with this c19 jab push. If the globalists have their way, private ownership of anything will be a thing of the past as they find ways of relieving humans of their properties. We all need to ask the Pleiadians and the Galactic Federation to please just tone down the frequencies coming from the reptilian humanoid hybrids hive controlling Moon. Galactic Federation please just do what you have to do in an effort to reprogram, calm them down and make them docile. For a change, turn the tables on them, the evil ones.

Why are human beings victims, and why did the Galactic Federation trap humans on Earth with the evil reptiles that have invaded our planet Earth? Can they be calmed down, way down? That would help us humans who have to live with them here on planet Earth. As the horribly destructive things they have been doing for over hundreds of years already is killing life on planet Earth. Seems to me our government might be in cahoots and taking orders from the evil reptiles in power and have sold us down the river of despair. To help us, the Pleiadians have many star-seeds here on Earth who have summoned the Galactic Federation and the Pleiadians to come to Earth to help and they came. And we are very glad they are here doing things to make life easier on humans. I have learned from ufologists Emirate Smith and David Wilcox video that the Galactic Federation brought to court members of the Illuminati and hopefully humans will see our human world conditions improve very soon.

There are now many starseeds from other star systems that are also on planet Earth to help. But I am only familiar with the Pleiadians, as I am a starseed from Alcyone of the Pleiades. Perhaps you are a starseed from the Pleiades, too.

One way to tell if you are a Pleiadian starseed is if you have anything in the sign of Taurus on your Astrological natal birth chart. To see if you are from the Pleiades, check if you have any asteroid, Sun, Moon, or any planet, or either the north or south node of the Moon in the sign of Taurus in your Astrological natal birth chart. If you do have even just one thing in the sign of Taurus, then you too are a Pleiadian starseed from the Pleiades. I only have the north node of the Moon in the sign of Taurus in the eighth house of contracts and working well with others. But it doesn't matter which house it is in, as long as you have something in the sign of Taurus, then you are from the Pleiades. And perhaps you too are here to help enlighten and awaken humans before it is too late. I guess that is all that it takes, one celestial unit of the universe in Taurus. Get TimePassages Pro for your smart phone, it's self-instructing and easy to follow, just put in your birth date, location and time of birth. Entering the time of birth makes the natal birth chart more accurate. If you do not know the exact time, use your intuition, or use high noon. I am sure that taking the time to draw your attention away from the everyday distractions of daily life to research, read, meditate, and connect with your passed loved ones and your guides will help you raise your consciousness and vibrations to the highest level. Believing in the process and yourself is the most important thing.

It is most important to love yourself and believe in yourself. And to have faith in yourself and your spiritual and psychic capabilities. It is important to believe that it is possible, and that it is necessary, in order to connect with the spiritual realm. Believing it is possible and recognizing your own inner knowing is key to success.

I think I have always felt I was not from here; always have enjoyed my alone time; never really feeling alone, as the Pleiadians have always made me feel special, safe and protected.

They connect with me telepathically. After a while you can learn to distinguish their messages from your own thoughts. They have always made me feel I was on a special mission and someone who was special and was being guided and protected. I thought that I was just born with a lot of common sense and intuition which can be a part of that too. However, it did not take me long to distinguish my own thoughts from my Pleiadian intuition messages that I was receiving, and I learned to keep them apart from my own thoughts. I believe there is a special feeling that comes along with their messages that give you a certain sense of knowing it is meant to be and is the right thing to do. It just feels right. Also at the time I may feel a certain knowing energy; a sensing if you will. The following is an example of Pleiadians guides helping me.

I was working the midnight to eight in the morning shift in downtown St. Louis, MO. I was leaving work driving in the right lane heading south. I was stopped at the stop light. A huge truck pulled up next to be in the left lane so I could not see what was coming from the east. The light turned green. Something made be notice that the truck to my left did not move. I took note of that. That was my guides trying to warn me. Then I think I felt the energy of the apparently concerned passenger in the truck to my left. As if he was thinking, "she better not go." Suddenly coming from the east, a huge older Buick came flying through the intersection as he ran his red light. If I had pulled forward as soon as my signal light changed from red to green, that huge Buick would have broadsided me right at my driver side door. I would surely have been killed as I was driving a small 1990 Mazda Miata, a small two seater sports car. I still thank my guides to this day.

Even with small things my Pleiadian guides help me. I lost my Kindle reader one day. I searched high and low around the house. Perhaps they helped me think to ask them for help, which I did. "Please help me find my Kindle," I asked. Within a second, I got a vision in my mind's eye of where the Kindle was. It was truly magical! They put that clairvoyant picture in my mind's eye. And when I saw the vision, I realized that I had left my Kindle in the front nylon pocket of the lawn chair. After the Pleiadians sent me the visual of the exact place where it was, I thanked them for helping me find it. What I had done was taken a lawn chair outside to get the warmth and energy from the sun, especially vitamin D and I learned that the sun also helps us get nourishing cholesterol up to our brains on our DNA level.

On another occasion, there are many. I just at the moment happen to recall this one. My Pleiadian guides also helped me find the back of my earring when I was getting dressed to go out one evening. I was running late so I asked them to help me. Within seconds they had me turn around and look down. They even enlarged the

23

vision of the back of the earring so I could spot it easier on my bedroom carpet. Soon as I spotted it, the vision of the back of the earring went back to its normal size. As I picked it up, I thanked them for helping me find it. It's good to thank them, they like that.

Chapter Two:

Convenient Inconveniences

I am so grateful for my Pleiadian family and my guides, they are blessings in this horrific world of blatant evil. I never take for granted my blessings and care from the Pleiadians. I have been fortunate to have inconveniences be more convenient. Like working the evening shift at the phone company, and able to park my 1990 Miata in the work garage, and noticing a flat tire, and able to call AAA, and they have a great dry lighted place to change my tire. I thanked my guides that it did not happen on the road. There would be nothing worse than sitting broken down alongside a busy road in the dark. I thank my Pleiadian guides. And I thank my Pleiadian guides for protecting me from reptilian humanoid hybrid brained men who see women as prey.

Recently on my road trip back to the southwest, I was leaving the motel room about five in the morning, when it was still dark. I had backed my car into the parking spot near the building and a door down from my motel room. I had locked the motel room door and was putting things in my car at passenger side front door. I make it a fast and convenient get away with only a couple of overnight bags and only opening the front passenger side door of my car. Out of the building a young tall dark-skinned man stopped behind my car and asked me a question.

"Ya got a light?" he asked in a stern voice.

"No, sorry," I replied, "I don't."

He took a couple steps away and stopped and looked at me.

"You don't have a light," he said with an accusing tone, as if I was lying. Of course, it is okay to speak that way to a stupid helpless woman, right? He would not have talked that way to a man! Just then behind me a car pulled up along side the building, it stopped and headlights were left on. So the headlights are shining on me. I think the tall dark stranger was about to head over toward my direction, that is until he saw the headlights of that car, then he walked on. I thanked my Pleiadian guides profusely for having that vehicle pull up next to the building exactly when it did, and leaving the lights on, which was enough to deter the idiot stranger. When I pulled up and turned right to leave, I saw that it was an SUV pulling a U-Haul. I imagined the guy went inside the building but left his lights on, or perhaps he was still sitting behind the wheel, I could not see inside the vehicle. Anyway, I was grateful that he pulled up and left the highlights on, which gave a sense of safety as if he might have been a security guard. As it was just enough to deter the mysterious tall dark stranger, who might have thought the vehicle was a security guard. The incident reminds me that some men appear not to like women and go after them as they see them as easy prey. Why is that? Why do some men have an evil reptilian brain, and are heartless, without a soul? I feel the need to refer back to the origin of slithering reptiles and how they came to be living underground on Earth, and why Earth is the prison planet that it is. Here's how it all began...

Twelve thousand, five hundred years ago, the reptiles were terrorizing the universe, blowing up planets and destroying everything in sight. So the Galactic Federation was formed and went after the reptiles. The reptiles set a booby trap and killed off half the members of the Galactic Federation. The remaining Galactic Federation members remained determined and chased after the evil reptiles. The reptiles were then on the run and decided to return to their home base on Lyra. But much to their surprise when they arrived at Lyra, they found their females had evidently had enough of them too and their evil male war-like behavior and decided to lock them out. So the reptiles fled to planet Earth and went underground. Since they had them in one place, the Galactic Federation immediately put the hallow Moon above Earth with a computer in it to hold Earth in the third dimension matrix. It was an effort to imprison the reptiles with the humans on Earth. This would have been just fine, if the reptiles had stayed underground where they were, as they had built underground cities and light rail systems to connect the cities. But, after a few thousand years they decided to rise and mingle with the humans on the surface of Earth.

"You can't go up there looking like that, why look at you, you are frightening," one reptile said to the other. The reptiles learned to hack the Moon's computer and learned how to steal DNA from white human males on Earth. Then they created the shape-shifting Reptilian Humanoid Hybrid male that can shift change to appear human. They appear human but did not inherit the heart and soul of a human. They are evil and hateful, psychopaths and sociopaths that can shape shift and pass as human men. Oh they know the things to say and do, and that's about it as they only know to hate, conquer and destroy. They pass pretty well as human males. But when angered their eyes can be seen to turn to yellow snake slit eyes. Two examples that were witnessed in modern times wanting a global rule NWO is poppy field guarding, George H. W. Bush, and more recently I learned about reptilian brain moron Mormon Warren Jeffs. Yes, I have watched Netflix's "Stay Sweet Pray and Obey." It's plain to see that evil satanic shape-shifting reptilian humanoid hybrid males such as these two examples are pure reptilian evil and they did not get the human heart moral compass or any benevolent human emotions, so they are soulless and ruthless to the core. And being without the love of a human heart and soul, they have no conscience so they do unthinkable things that humans could not possibly comprehend doing. Look around, you will find they have ruthlessly scratched and clawed their way into high positions of corporations and governments. Also, when the reptiles hacked the Moon's computer, they tweaked it to control the human males; that is, the reptilian humanoid hybrids they created, so they are pretty much the same worldwide, but some are even more evil and without conscience. I am so happy to be from the Pleiades and able to see the horrid atrocities that are happening and have my Pleiadian guides guarding and watching over me.

So I have been very fortunate. I believe my guides have always helped to protect me and have things happen at convenient places like when my 12volt battery went dead on my 2016 Prius. It happened at home and when I had no appointment or place where I had to be. I called AAA, he jumped it, got my car started and told me where the O'Reilly's auto store was and that it was open on Sundays. I drove right there and did not turn my car off, until I knew that they had the correct battery for my car. See how convenient my wonderful Pleiadian guides made my inconvenience? Here is another example I found to be reaffirming that connected me to my Pleiadian family.

I found this to be very interesting and Pleiadian starseed life affirming. I read somewhere that if your past and present home addresses each add up to the number seven then you are a Pleiadian from the Pleiades. Well, I have had three addresses since 1987 (btw,1987=25 and 2+5=7) and each address numbers add up to the number seven. The first one, that I presently rent in the SW address adds up to seven (13021=7). My condo address

I presently own in St. Louis adds up to seven (9133=16 and 1+6=7). And the home I owned prior to moving to the St. Louis address, in Belleville, IL (1402=7) added up to the number seven. Each of the residence's addresses add up to the number seven. Guess they were trying to tell me all along that I am from the Pleiades. Pretty amazing, isn't it. Of course, my Pleiadian guides led me to that number seven clue information. Get it! See how they can arrange things in your life and then give you information relating to those things they want you to know. Oh and of course, they had to have me learn that if your addresses each add up to the number seven you are from the Pleiades, so they directed me to learn that and so much more.

Chapter Three:

Guided and Protected

My passed soul spiritual guides (I will introduce them later) and the Pleiadians have protected me through the years from illness, accidents, marriage, and from having children. Funny? Yes marriage and children. From a very young age when I realized that society norms were very much geared to and in favor of white males. Yes, can't you tell that reptilian humanoid hybrid males planned the world to be patriarchal to serve themselves, of course?

They even rewrote the Bible to suit themselves. They showed their true selfish self-serving, egotistical, narcissistic agenda by grouping their very own white women, along with all the other races, to be considered second class citizens. This was a clue to me that white males were reptilian humanoid hybrids created by the evil reptiles lurking in caves underground. The reptilian humanoid hybrid males rewrote the Bible to suit themselves which included the story of Adam and Eve in the Garden of Eden, where the serpent tempted

Eve and then she tempted Adam with the forbidden apple. So it was her fault that they were cast out of the garden of Eden. Therefore women had to be punished by painful childbirth according to scripture. Sure, blame the woman! I believe that since the reptilian females locked the reptile males out of Lyra, that all females, including white human females were hated by the reptilian humanoid hybrid white males and their reptilian masters hiding underground. The Pleiadians had me see the darkness of the patriarchal society. So I was not to bear children or to marry as being a starseed, the Pleiadians did not wish for me to create Earthly karma.

I was to remain a free spirit and so I wanted no part of living under a man's thumb in a patriarchal society. I am gifted to be a Pleiadian starseed. Perhaps you are one too. There is a list to test yourself, to see if you are a starseed. Some things on the list are, having empathy, needing alone time. Able to enjoy social events, but always ready to be back home again. Being put on spiritual soul sharing missions that may include falling in love with troubled souls. Starseeds can easily fall into traps because they have a generous loving heart easily giving their power away to please others. I have never wanted children or to be married, as I believe coming from the Pleiades, they do not want us starseeds to create karma where we may want to reincarnate back here again on planet Earth. I believe many starseeds do not get married or have children as to not create karma. Karma keeps you reincarnating back to the third dimension, and they do not want me to do that. Actually, flying solo, cherishing alone time especially in nature, is very common among starseeds. We love to socialize but then we need our recharging alone time too. Being a starseed from Alcyone of the Pleiades I spend much time mediating to raise my vibrations up to connect with the good spirits across the veil. The veil is thinning because the earth is in the fifth dimension now, so if we are prepared then seeing ghosts and spirits and aliens will not be such a shock to us. As the veil between Earth and the spirit world thins, we will be more connected with the other side. It makes spiritual connections for starseeds who are mediums a little easier.

I recently had a negative spirit experience as I returned from a visit to the Midwest back to my southwest home. And I do not normally see negative spirits. But when I returned to my southwest home I saw a dark, soulless, cluster of skulls in my mind's eye. I merely said, "Go away now," and they left. Then for good measure I burned sage and walked through each room fanning out smoke with my hand. I never saw them again. I think they were left over negative energy from the adjacent condo that had mentally troubled occupants evicted while I was away. Evil spirit is not to be feared. When I do my mediumship readings, to prepare I sit in silence, mediate and raise my vibrations. I merely say, "Only the good spirits come forward." No need to worry about dealing with the negative that may be lurking. As a medium I raise my vibrations, as I instruct the potential sitter to do the same, The sitter and I raise our vibrations and the spirits lower their vibrations in order to connect with us during a mediumship reading.

Chapter Four:

On being a Medium

In order to connect with spirit, the medium and the sitter need to raise their vibrations and the passed over soul spirit needs to lower theirs for we three to connect. So that I as the medium am a mere conduit between the sitter and the soul spirit. The spirit gives me their information to pass on to the sitter, then I deliver the messages to the sitter. I usually sit across from the sitter; it works just as well on zoom, by the way. I close my eyes, lean slightly forward usually to the sitter's left shoulder a bit. I keep my eyes closed. I keep my mind open. I push my own thoughts to the side. I act as a mere conduit. I think of nothing and wait. Usually within a few seconds a spirit comes forward. If you are ever afraid of being a medium and having negative dark spirits come forth, just begin by saying to yourself, "only the good spirits come forward," and that is all you need to do. So I have my eyes closed and then usually within a couple of seconds, I begin to clairvoyantly see spirit, I get an image. I'll never forget my first actual mediumship reading. It was magical. After the reading, I felt high as a kite and so connected with my Pleiadians, my guides, with past souls, and even the Moon and the stars as I drove home that evening.

It brings tears to my eyes just thinking about it. In my first reading image, I saw a soldier dressed in casual military clothes of khaki pants and shirt, military style, and he had one of those small army crown hats, the kind they fold across their belt. I got that he was a WWII war veteran. He was happy and proud to have served his country, He was a returning war veteran. He loved his family and was proud to protect them during a time of war. I said, "I see a grandfather or great-grandfather figure and he loves and watches over you all the time. He is very proud of the young responsible woman you have become." I then saw a red apple. I told her it seems he was standing in his bedroom, at home, like in front of an open closet. I began to tell her everything that I saw before I opened my eyes, because I do not want the sitter's facial expressions to affect my delivery of messages to her. And I told her everything. I even mentioned that I saw a red apple.

"Oh, that is my great grandfather, he was a teacher before he went into the army to fight WWII. He loved getting apples from the students." The sitter smiled with tears in her eyes. I teared up too, which is very easy to do working with spirit as they are pure love, and they touch your heart, and you touch theirs. I remember many of my readings. In St. Louis, I studied and practiced mediumship under Julia Marie. One evening at a practice galley she mentioned that the grand dame of Mediumship of England was to conduct a mediumship seminar in Chicago soon. It was very rare for Mavis Pittalla to be in the United States and only a few hours away. I was determined to go. I figured the Pleiadians had spoken through my instructor so I would learn Mavis Pittalla was coming to a city near me. I immediately registered for the seminar which was just a few weeks away.

Chapter Five:

Mavis Pittalla in Chicago

I was so excited in October of 2017, while at a practice intuition medium ship galley, to learn that Mavis Pittalla, the grand dame of mediumship of England and her partner, Jane, would be conducting a four-day mediumship seminar in Chicago, IL. I couldn't wait to get there, I knew the drive and the event was meant to be for me because my guides and Pleiadian family had me learn about the event. I knew the drive from St. Louis to Schaumburg, IL, near Chicago would go smoothly, and it did.

I could not wait to get there. I was so excited to meet and study with Mavis Pittalla whom I had heard so much about. I just knew it would be a magical, spiritual, and a once-in-a-lifetime wonderful experience.

Finally, the day of the seminar arrived. I was eager to begin. There were sixty-four of us in the class. It was grand to be with so many likeminded souls. Mavis had us split into groups of three for practice, one to be the recorder, one the sitter, and one the medium. Before we began Mavis stood before to join us in a group prayer, oddly enough she stood close to we three in our group as we were in the back of the classroom. After the prayer, the sitter in my threesome asked me and the woman who was to be the recorder if we felt Mavis' prayer in our hearts. And yes, all three of us did. It was like a strong soul feeling of love. Much like I feel now for Steve's cousin, a deep soul love connection, after I delivered Steve's messages to her. More about that later. After the heart-felt prayer, we began our practice readings.

We three sat at a small square table. To begin, I sat across from the sitter, closed my eyes, cleared my thoughts, imagined my mind was a tunnel, or a conduit, without any thought interference. I began to see something clairvoyantly in my mind's eyes. Again about the left shoulder of the sitter. With my eyes closed to omit distraction, I saw a young woman, dark hair flying in her face, bent over, as if taking a dive off something. She had the look of surprise and fear as she was going over something. I saw water. I saw the young woman was a little mischievous in high school but had a male teacher who was patient with her and had her under his wing. She was troubled and she lived life in the fast lane, as if somehow she sensed that her life would be cut short. When I saw the water I thought she may have driven her car in a ditch, but I saw no car, she was on something else, perhaps a boat. She came forward for the sitter because he was grateful that the sitter was always kind to her, and she enjoyed their friendship. Maybe she was going over a boat railing. Keeping my eyes closed, so not to be distracted by her expressions, I told the sitter what I received. The sitter said the image I received was that of her friend, who went on a houseboat party out on a lake one evening, and when the boat returned to the dock she was not on it. So they looked for her, through the night, and the next morning they found her body near the shoreline. I guess that was the ditch I thought I saw, as I saw a brush covered and slightly wooded shoreline. Every once in a while I still can see that imagine of her going overboard, I have named her the Lady of the Lake. This just made me cry. She made me cry.

Just thinking and connecting with spirit will touch your heart. They relay their gratitude, and I know I hit home with them when they make me feel like crying. The images and the messages of readings can linger and stay with you. I always say only the good spirits can come forward, and I say that when I mediate and before a reading.

Mavis had a way to push us a little to our limits. For me she had me give a *power to the spirit* life coach speech. It was in the spur of the moment and as I stood before the classroom of sixty-four students, I saw all of them looking at me with their full attention. Their faces were smiling, and their eyes seemed eager to hear what I had to say. In retrospect, I think the Pleiadians created those smiling, eager-to-learn faces to give me confidence, because they all looked exactly the same to me.

"Your word is *'courage'*," Mavis said.

I had to think fast, on my feet, in the moment. I did not even have time to get nervous as I gathered my thoughts and asked the Pleiadians to help me. As I peered out over the classroom of sixty-four students I slowly began. To my comfort and amazement, for a moment their faces all smiled with the same enthusiasm. I saw that I had everyone's undivided attention, as they all looked at me with bright eyes, and smiling faces appearing eager to hear what I had to say. I believe my Pleiadian family and my guides, Rosie and Emma gave me that gift to build up my own courage and spark some interesting points for me to give to the classroom.

I began by saying that it takes courage to be a medium, courage to face some family members and friends' disbelief in the process. How many of us mediums were raised in the strict Catholic religion or other ideals which frown on such spiritual connections? Many are doubters, naysayers needing proof. I have always thought it takes courage to face the truth or to confront the teachings of what religion tells you is right, or wrong. It takes courage to have faith in the spirit world, in your god. So then why not have courage to connect with the divine of the spirit with mediumship readings? It takes courage, faith and trust to believe in the spiritual unknown. For example, there were parents who lost a son. Of course the parents were devastated and missed their son terribly. They wanted to know he was okay. So they contacted a medium. But the father needed a sign from his passed over son. After the mediumship reading, he was a little more hopeful in his belief of the messages delivered during the reading. Subconsciously, however, he was still doubtful. To his and his wife's amazement, when they returned home, they were greeted with flashing ceiling lights in the kitchen. To his wife that was an obvious loving sign from their son passed over across the veil. But, what does the doubting, I-need-proof, man do? He calls a electrician! I bet the spirit of his son was thinking that is just the way dad is. Why do you think the son, made the sign from himself to his father so dramatic? His son was probably insulted that his dad still did not believe in him or in his spiritual powers.

Naysayers, in my opinion, only short-change themselves and that is where it takes courage for not only the medium but for the sitter too. Why is it so difficult to believe in spiritual messages? Duh! We believe the crap the media dishes out, and we believe the pharmaceutical companies that have hijacked our very own government. We follow the leader and fall in line to roll up our sleeves to a fake virus and dangerous jabs that are filled with all sorts of foreign items that are toxic to the human body. Foreign and toxic to the body ingredients such polyethylene glycol (so nano particles do not stick together), formaldehyde (for preservation) snake venom for the spike protein. Snake venom you say? Yes, I said snake venom. I guess just because reptiles are running the show and that is their secret signature ingredient. Probably other ingredients of mercury and aluminum too, just added for good measure. I am so grateful my Pleiadian family has protected and guided me.

My Pleiadian guides were adamant about me not getting the jab, as they directed me through my gut feelings and my intuition to say, an affirmative, "No." My intuition said no to the jabs. My guides would have had me kicking and screaming not to get that jab if needed. And, if I ever need a doctor, I will go a holistic doctor, certainly not one of conflict-of-interest pill pushing, jab pushing, for-profit. It is clear to me that my guides and the Pleiadians do not want anything foreign to my body. According to my research and holistic thinking, their pills are only band aids, never a healing cure. And many pills are addictive heroin based, covering up the real problem with mere pain pills.

Can you tell that I have watched the documentary series on Netflix called *"Painkiller"* all about Oxycontin. May I suggest you watch it. My Pleiadian guides had me watch it to confirm suspicions that I already had about our for-profit drug and allopathic health care system. Purdue took Heroin, a schedule two narcotic, off the streets, made it a twelve hour pain pill, and made it legal by paying off the government guy who refused to approve it. Well, not until the price was right. So where is our government protection? That guy worked for the FDA.

Where is the moral compass? So they can't be fully human! Where is the honor and integrity? Does power and money really mean that much? Millions became so addicted to Oxycontin that they were robbing and stealing and breaking the law to get their heroin fix, legal heroin fix! Yes, black tar heroin. There are more petroleum oil products, they are everywhere.

Pleiadians have guided and led me to learn that certain chemicals like petroleum-based products are in many products, such as Polyethylene Glycol, which is antifreeze. Yes, I said antifreeze! Remember the warnings on television years back. You should be careful when adding toxic antifreeze to winterize your car's radiator, not to spill it, as it is toxic but sweet, and your dog may come along and lick it up off the driveway. Guess they were more worried about dogs' health than humans' health, because now it is in everything. Look at the back of a box of sinus aid Sudafed PE. The ingredients say aluminum and polyethylene glycol. Also go to the pastry department of your grocery store, where they do the baking. Pick up something moist like a pound cake, read the label. Polyethylene glycol, right? It's made from petroleum. Wow, talk about greed! Oil has to be in everything. So you don't think evil is running the show?

Evil lurks in high places. John Warner III said he once asked a military general, "Just who is really running the government?"

"The reptiles," the General replied.

When I heard this, I thought why do the generals tolerate this? Shouldn't they be protecting the citizens and the Constitution? Allowing toxins in the community and lying about their safety is an act of treason, is it not? Our government and all positions of power have been invaded by evil, without souls or consciousness, entities, it sure seems like it to me, anyway. I mean generals have seen Poppy George Bush's eyes turn to yellow snake eye vertical slits when he became angry. I guess the generals are mind-controlled puppets. I believe Netflix has tried to give us hints with some of their productions. On Netflix watch the series: *Keep Sweet, Pray and Obey* all about Warren Jeffs seventy-five wives. And they did not say this at all in the series, but, what else can one believe. Is this a women for babies for reptiles scheme? It makes one wonder. One of Jeff's many brothers, as Warren Jeff's father had seventy-five wives too, had his own opinion.

"They treat women like cattle," the brother said. The saying is, the more wives, the higher the place in heaven. Really? Well, here is my Pleiadian mind summation. Why seventy-five young baby producing age wives? Perhaps the truth is that evil reptiles living underground in caves, have a taste for human flesh, the younger the better. The more frightened the better. Now this was not said in the series. I read in Len Kasten books that reptiles have a taste for baby flesh. Just watch it and come to your own conclusions. I suggest you watch it, each part, all the way through, because either at the end of Part Two, or Part three, you will see an angry Warren Jeff's eyes turn to yellow snake eye slits of pure evil. He's a reptilian humanoid hybrid, just like old man Bush was. Come to your own conclusions.

I realize that this bazaar stuff may be hard to comprehend. The reptiles count on that, and that contributes to their clandestine evil ways, as they carry on as the slithering reptiles that they are. Seems their secret signature ingredient in the jabs was of all things, snake venom. Isn't that a clue that underground reptiles are lurking and have reptilian humanoid hybrid males in high places doing their bidding?

I was appalled when I first heard that snake venom was in the c19 jabs, probably in flu jabs too. I could not believe what I was reading. All along I was giving the drug companies the benefit of a doubt. Thinking some labs were cleaner or managed better than others and accidents can happen, like making the vaccines serums maybe too strong. My Pleiadian guides have led me to the books and internet sites that they wanted me to see and learn from. As of July 2023, when I learned about the snake venom from the Jonathan Otto and Dr. Bryan Ardis sites, I believe my Pleiadian guides gave me the idea to begin a *DianneTheMedium* podcast on PodBean.

I feel the Pleiadians have me on planet Earth at this important time in the history of humankind for a reason which is to use our internet resources to spread the word to enlighten and awaken and become aware and whenever possible to go the holistic and organic way. They have also had me learn from Len Kasten books and shows on GAIA and other media to piece together just how it all came to be this way. They also help me write my books. I have written and published eight fictional books so far.

My Pleiadian guides are the best. When I wrote *Pleasant View* they helped me find the perfect poison to use. You see Pleasant View retirement center offered to manage and invest their residents investment portfolios, and they cooked for them too. I got the idea in the first place to write the book, when my friend said her neighbor was selling her place and moving to a retirement center. She said the retirement center took care of everything, even managing her investment portfolio.

"And they cook for them, too?" I asked. So that was when I got the idea for the book. In the book, the retirement center owner's wife just happened to be very greedy. So it was a lethal recipe set for disaster. While writing the book I went to the library to do some research, I was looking for a poison to use for the book. Lo and behold, I found it in the first newspaper I picked up which was *USA Today*. I saw an article about a man who hunted for mushrooms in northern California. The countryside was plentiful and he gathered many. Being a nice guy, he took some to the retirement home where his folks lived and gave them to the cook. Well, moral of the story, make sure you know your mushrooms, as most people got sick and some even died from the toxicity of those mushrooms. The article gave the technical name for the bad mushrooms. So I thanked my Pleiadian guides for the idea to use mushrooms in my story. It was perfect!

I believe my Pleiadian friends helped me with all my books. When I wrote *Verda*, which is all about a life-threatening, but turns out to be fake virus, and the real threat was the toxic jabs. Sound familiar? I put the story on a fictional planet called Verda. On Verda where evil shape-shifting to appear as humans, reptiles, are in control. And the Pleiadians, of course, come to the rescue. My Pleiadian guides have helped me write about these issues. They also helped me find a podcast outlet in PodBean for my *DianneTheMedium* podcast. Check it out.

They gave me the podcast idea, as did Mavis Pittalla when she told me I should write books, which I was already doing, and I should be a life coach speaker, thus the podcasts. So, I talk about my thoughts, what I have read and learned regarding current events. Listen to *DianneTheMedium* on PodBean. It is apparent to me that evil lurks in powerful positions and that reptilian humanoid hybrid males have scratched and clawed their way into powerful positions. Don't you get the feeling that humans beings are mere victims living here on planet Earth and need help from the Galactic Federation to come and help us.

When passed soul spirits come through during my mediumship in person or zoom readings, I like to invite them to feel free to inform me and the sitter as to what they see happening on Earth from their point of view from the other side of the veil. Mediumship readings can be very magical for the sprit that comes forward, for the sitter and for me.

Chapter Six:

Zoom Reading

On my website, DianneTheMedium.com contact page, people can send me an email requesting a free zoom mediumship reading. It works just as well over zoom. I received an email one day from someone saying something drew her to my website. I figured she was my guide Rosie, more about her later. Or later on after the reading, I wondered if maybe the sitter's grandfather, who came through, drew her to my website. I emailed the potential sitter back, and we set up a day and time for her free zoom mediumship reading. I said I usually allow about an hour, so set aside an hour in your schedule. The day came for our zoom meeting.

She was a young and attractive woman with dark hair. I explained to her that I close my eyes to not be distracted. Again, I saw clairvoyantly near her left shoulder, an image of an older gentleman. I got that she had taken care of him before he passed, and he was most grateful for that. He let me know she was considering a baby, but perhaps the man she was seeing did not want children, and she was nearing the age where she needed to make a decision. And grandfather was right there to help her make a decision as he spoke through me to her.

"This is the 21st century," her grandfather said, "if you have the means, you go ahead and have that little girl on your own," which I passed on to her. And then I told her of an image he presented me with, where I saw her sitting with a little girl about two or three. The little girl had long dark hair like her mother and was the spitting image of her mother. With my eyes closed I told her exactly what I got and what I saw. She said that was her grandfather and that she did take care of him before he passed. She was moved to tears as I was, especially when I told her about the mother and little girl image. So readings can be very magical and rewarding for the spirit that comes forward, the sitter, and for the medium.

Chapter Seven:

Dogs

When I began studying intuition and meditation for mediumship practice, I began noticing that dogs paused in their tracks, to stop and stare at me. It made their owners stand and wait until I caught up to them. Evidently, they were seeing something in me-- or who knows maybe a spirit around me. Perhaps I had entered the fifth dimension, or were my guides and Pleiadians having fun with me? No matter, I loved the insight and the soul connection with animals. On a walk in the neighborhood, I would come across someone walking their dog about a block ahead of me and for some reason, perhaps the dog felt my looking at him, the dog would turn around at look at me. So if the dog turned around to see me, they would stop in their tracks and wait for me to catch up to them. And something made the dog turn around in the first place, right? Like my eyes on them? Did they feel me looking at them? I saw what was going on and hastened my steps because their owners were having to stand there and wait. Sometimes I found myself apologizing to the owners.

"I'll come over and say hi," I always said and when I caught up to them, I would always bend down, pet and talk to the dog and then the dog was ready to move on with his owner once again. This happened often when I was out for a walk.

One day a dog riding in the back seat of an SUV, saw me and got rather daring. I was jogging down the sidewalk heading to a park. I was on the east side of the street running toward the south, and there was a truck waiting to pull out onto McKnight, a rather busy street, but he just sat there, and I wondered why. And then I saw a car to his left on McKnight, and she had stopped dead right in the street. I felt something going on behind me. I turned to look over my right shoulder and saw a southbound SUV on McKnight stopped in the street, his driver side door was open and he was getting out, his back seat window was half way down. Then I realized the dog had jumped out that backseat window to come run with me on the sidewalk. I turned around, I saw that he was trying to catch up with me. By then the woman had pulled up.

"Is the dog okay?" she asked. "He landed really hard when he jumped out the window of the car." And yes, the dog jumped out of a moving SUV. Grant you, the SUV was moving south on McKnight probably close to 30 mph when the dog jumped out the back seat window and crossed the other traffic lane to come run with me. It was just a good thing a car wasn't right there to hit the dog. What that dog saw in me I do not know. I realized the dog jumped out of a moving vehicle to come join me in my run down the sidewalk. Of course, I felt bad for the dog and knelt down next to him to talk to him and to pet him.

"He's never done anything like that before," the puzzled and concerned owner said.

Of course, I felt slightly other worldly after that, and even more connected with my Pleiadian guides and my guides Rosie and Emma. In December 2019, the spirit of Steve introduced himself to me, and now he is my guide too. More about them later.

Another dog story. On another day I was in front of our condo complex club house getting signatures on a petition to get medical marijuana on the ballot. It was an election day. I stood on the sidewalk greeting voters and asking them if they wished to sign the petition, and the majority of them did. While I stood there between speaking to potential signers, I noticed a young woman across the street was trying to walk her dog; but the dog stood frozen in place staring at me from across the street. The young woman appeared to be in a hurry, as if she had to be somewhere; it looked to me that she had to get to work or some place important. The dog was between two cars near the curb, and it appeared he wasn't budging as she tugged on his leash. The dog just stood and stared at me. Finally I yelled to her.

"I'll come over there and say a quick hi," I said. I waited for a car to pass and then hurried and walked across the street. The dog was not moving and still staring at me. I bent over and spoke nicely and petted the dog. Finally it seemed he was satisfied with my visit.

"Okay then off you go," I said, "enjoy your walk," and then the dog happily went on with his owner. "Sorry," I told her, "I do not know why that happens. I have no idea what they see in me." She merely smiled and they went on their way.

Isn't that too strange. I have no idea what those dogs saw in me. All I know is that I had been sitting in power, that is what mediums call meditating, to raise my consciousness and vibrations for my mediumship practice to enhance my ability to connect with the other side. My mediumship instructor was puzzled when I told her the stories of the dogs and when I began seeing more and more dogs come forward at mediumship galley groups readings.

"Are you sure you are not from Sirius," Julia Marie asked one evening. I wondered: was it my passed over Rottweiler dog, Emma, seeing me through them and wanting to say hi, and for me to pet her through them. I think maybe it might have been my passed Rottweiler Emma coming through via the dogs. But Emma really did me good one day.

It was late January, about five or six years after she passed. She was fifteen. She was the best dog and so smart, like a human. So much so, I would tell her she was so intelligent, rather than smart. She was a gift.

Chapter Eight:

Emma

In 1995 my best friend and co-worker and I bought a log home on the bluffs overlooking the Mississippi River valley in Illinois. Her nephew had a girlfriend whose dog did not get along with her nephew's dog. They wanted to know if we would take about six-year-old Emma, a Rottweiler. They said she was very well trained. Well, we thought with a name like Emma, she must be a sweetie. She was sweet and very very smart. I used to tell her that she was very intelligent. She was a joy to have around, and we felt extra safe having her with us at night living in the woods on the bluff in our log cabin. When I was working days and my friend was working evenings, Emma knew just about when my friend would be coming home from work, and she wanted outside. She sat at the top of the driveway and waited. She usually wanted out about twenty minutes before my friend was due home. Amazing how they can sense time. She was very well trained. She would never go through a doorway, she would hesitate until

I told her it was okay to go. She would never pass me or race ahead walking up or down steps. She always walked along side of me. She was a great dog, we had her until she was about fifteen years old when she passed. I thought about her often, and I know she is now my guide, my protector guide.

It was a beautiful sunny late January day, and I think Emma planned this, just like she had me get the sudden urge to go for a walk. I decided I needed a destination, I'm sure she helped with that too. I'll just walk about a mile to Walgreens I thought. So I did. When I got to Walgreens, I thought I would walk toward the far end to the photo camera department and maybe get something to drink. About three quarters of the way there, I felt eyes on me coming from over my right shoulder, but the eyes felt rather as if coming from a high place. Must be a very tall person, I thought. As soon as I turned and looked where I felt the eyes coming from, I saw a little, about eight inches tall, black and brown Rottweiler stuffed puppy on the top shelf. No wonder the eyes felt high. Emma! I rushed right over, reached up and got her down, and hugged her. And trust me, I wanted to cry right there in Walgreens when I saw that she had a Valentine's Day rose in her mouth for me. Makes me cry as I write this. What a loving gift! She travels with me between St. Louis and Sedona. I got her a pal puppy and they both sit on the bed pillows guarding the house when I am out running errands, for hike, walk, or bike ride. See how spirit can connect with you from the other side, even a dog's spirit through a stuffed animal. Pretty magical, isn't it? Makes me cry just thinking about it.

There had been other times when I felt animal eyes on me, and it made me look up at them, like birds sitting under an overpass, or a cat looking down at me from an open second story window. Emma was the best dog. Some people say their dogs are smart, I say that Emma was intelligent, like a human. I only had to tell her something just one time.

For example, when we moved from the log home back into the condo, she would want to go outside in the back. I would peer out the patio door and watch her, and she actually tried to slip away without me noticing. She walked in slow motion as she was sneaking off to the neighbor's condo. Emma knew that the neighbor down the way put food out for the wild cats that lived along the railroad in the deep ditch a few yards from our back patios. Then after a few minutes she would come back, the same way. She scratched on the patio screen to get back in. And I just had to correct her one time.

"Emma, no scratch here," I said as I took her right paw in my hand and showed her not to scratch on the screen. 'It's okay to scratch over here," I said as I then took her paw and padded it against the wooden frame of the patio door. She never forgot after that.

I boosted her up on to the backseat of my RAV4 one time and she expected me to boost her butt up, each time there after when we were going for a ride. Riding in the car was a big thing to Emma. She loved her halter that fastened around her through the seat belt, as it held her steady. If she felt the ride was not long enough, she acted like she did not want to get out of the car. There were other times when I got to see her unique human-like personality.

There were six of us on a hike one day when we came to a fallen tree we had to step over. It was not that big, but appeared to be a challenge to Emma. I knew she could do it. So I took her right paw and showed her. I stepped over the log myself, to show her it could be done. Finally, she proudly braved it, and we went on. On the way back, we purposely headed our hike a few feet around the fallen tree, but Emma headed for the fallen tree as if she wanted to show us that she could now step over that log in the trail. I miss her. She is gone physically but definitely here with me in spirit.

It's a blessing to be able to connect with animals; it's a refreshing sign that I am in the fifth dimension where we are soul to soul connected by the love of the universe.

One time I was in a park jogging, approaching an overpass on the trail. I felt eyes on me and when I looked up a bird sat quietly looking down at me. I thought, *I wonder who that is?* It felt magical whoever it was.

Another time I was walking on the sidewalk close to home, when I felt eyes on me. I looked up to see a cat in an open second floor window looking down at me. Pretty cool. Birds have a way of connecting with me too. This bird story is magical and is the best yet.

Chapter Nine:

A Bird Named Forest Park

On October 1, 2023, last fall, I was home in St Louis, and I rode my bike to Forest Park. I love Forest Park. It's on a vortex that runs from the North Pole through St. Louis down to the Gulf of Mexico. There are many, like spokes on a wagon wheel originating near the North Pole. There is one spoke through Flagstaff and Sedona to Mexico., One through Santa Fe, NM, then another through St. Louis, and still another on the East coast from North Pole through Pennsylvia, down to Raleigh, NC. I believe there is a vortex where there are lots of crystals and gems in the ground. So it feels magical to me.

As I was saying, I rode my bike to Forest Park, and I found a nice bench next to a rocky stream. I was wearing my helmet, biking glasses and a colorful biking jersey. I had my road bike propped against the back of an eight-foot-long bench with middle arm rest. I was sitting on the right end with my iPhone on PodBean doing my

DianneTheMedium podcast, when I began to notice a bird sitting on the back of the bench, then on the far arm rest, then the middle arm rest, just hanging around. I thought maybe it was fascinated with the bright colors of my biking jersey or my helmet or my rather large biking sunglasses. It fluttered its wings against my sunglasses several times, flew away then returned to do it again four or five times. I thought the bird could be someone's parakeet that got out of its cage and escaped the house it lived in. It sat behind me on the bench rail, and I felt its feathers flutter against the back of my neck. I spoke of the bird during my podcast. After a bit it dawned on me to stop the podcast and do a video of the bird. On the video I named the bird Forest Park. I have the video on my Facebook profile page which is open to the public and the podcast is at *DianneTheMedium* at PodBean dated October 1, 2023. You can hear me decide to name the bird as it sat on my bicycle seat, then sat on the back of the bench near my shoulder, and then he actually sat on my shoulder. Where I turned to him and spoke to him.

"I think I'll name you Forest Park," I said. The little bird was not afraid of me as I turned and spoke to it. Then it jumped onto my shoulder again, made a gesture as if to peck me sweetly on the cheek, sat back on my shoulder just for a second, and then flew off. Sadly to my disappointment, it did not come back. I actually rode my bike back to Forest Park the next day about the same time and sat on the same bench just in case the little bird might come back again, but sadly it did not.

A friend saw the video and said it was a Phoebe bird. I wondered, who was that? Was it the spirit of Steve I wondered? So here is the Steve story, but first I have to introduce my guide Rosie to you.

Chapter Ten:

My Guide Rosie

When I was in my late twenties or early thirties, I had a many friends; we called ourselves, "The Group." Like what's the group doing tonight? We hung out in a thirty-six-lane bowling alley with a nice big lounge that hosted bands with a small dance floor. It was our regular hangout where people knew to find us. There were always bands. We were friendly, single, and the group grew and spilled over into house parties. It never failed at house parties later in the evening, my friend Rosie and I would end up at the ice chest getting a beer, closing the lid and sitting down on it. I remember it was blue ice chest with a white lid about thirty inches wide. Anyway, we had little butts and we fit on it just fine.

"Come on, Dianne," Rosie would say, "let's sit and talk." And so we did after we each got a beer from the ice chest, closed the lid and sat down on it. I always enjoyed our conversations which usually ended up talking about metaphysical stuff. She had a sweet angelic way about her, and I always enjoyed her company and our conversations. Little did I know that those moments would come back to me in late 2017. Back then, in our thirties in the 1980s, she would ask me metaphysical questions. Maybe she sensed something in me too. Looking back, maybe it was a prelude to our futures as sadly she got cancer and passed a few years later. Several years later I became a medium.

In 2017, in a mediumship galley, with Julia Marie, my mediumship instructor, Rosie came through and introduced herself to me. It made me remember those evenings at those house parties sitting on the ice chest when she asked me questions. Perhaps her guides and her intuition were preparing her for her future and evidently mine too.

"Do you believe in life after death?" she asked me as we drank our beer and shared our seat on the ice chest.

"Yes, I do, believe," I said. "I believe that we are spiritual beings here on Earth to experience life as human beings."

"Or do you believe when you die that's it, its final?" she asked.

"I believe, only our bodies die, that our souls live on," I said.

Funny how those moments with Rosie stuck in my mind after all those years. You see there was a reason, she and I had those conversations in the first place. Either it was our guides or the Pleiadians connecting and preparing both of us or giving us a hint of what was to come in the future. Sadly, my good friend Rosie passed in her late thirties from ovarian cancer. When she was very ill near the end, I could not bring myself to go see her. And somehow my guides had me feel that that was okay. And years later I figured out why. Neither my Pleiadian guides nor Rosie wanted me to remember her that way. Because years later she would be reintroducing herself in spirit to me. And when she did, I pictured her as she was when she and I sat on that ice chest. And so it came to be.

And close to thirty years later, it was around early 2017 I think, I was at Mystic Valley Book and Gem store on Manchester in St. Louis attending a mediumship galley with instructor Julia Marie. Now this is after experiencing those dogs waiting for me and Emma's stuffed puppy eyes on me. There were at least seven of us there in the galley, Julia Marie was going to read each one of us. I was last in line. When Julia Marie got to me, I sat patiently waiting to see who would come forward.

"I see three or thirty-three," she said.

I was trying to think who died three years ago, or thirty-three years ago. Anyway, as I sat there pondering.

"You are the medium. I will bring them forward," Julia Marie suddenly said this to me, for the spirit that was coming forward to her and to me at the same time. Suddenly I saw the name Rosie spelled out in puffed of white clouds against a blue-sky background. "Rosie!" I was tickled and immediately envisioned the only Rosie I have ever known and that was my good friend Rosie. I immediately remembered our wonderful conversations.

"Do you believe in life after death?" she would ask. "Or do you believe when your dead you are dead?"

"I believe in life after death," I would say, "and when we die only our bodies die but our souls live on."

I recalled those moments together talking metaphysical as we shared the ice chest seat; they remain very meaningful. She agreed as she believed that when our bodies die that our souls live on. I wondered if there was a pattern or a reason I remembered Rosie and our chats about the spirit world. Did those moments remain in my memory of those evenings for a reason? Perhaps to be recalled years later after she passed when she introduced herself to me during that psychic medium galley at Mystic Valley Gem and Book store in 2017. See how the spirit world works? She passed around 1990 and connected with me from the other side in 2017. I believe there is no tracked sense of time on the other side; not like we track it here on Earth.

Rosie is my guide now and she did bring a passed spirit forward in 2018, a spirit named Steve. He passed in an auto accident at age fifteen in 1969. See how time is not really a factor from the other side of the veil, which makes it that much more spectacular. I believe the souls we meet and make contact with along the way during our paths in life have been written into reality long before events occur, and then they may come back around again. For example, Rosie reconnecting with me years after she passed. I believe all the above is the reason I am a medium. I guess back when the universe or the Pleiadians knew someday I would become a psychic medium, Rosie would be my guide, and Rosie would help bring them (only the good spirits) forward.

See how all life events can be connected and why they happen and why you remember them for a later life's event. Rosie always appeared angelic to me. I was glad I had an old photo album with several pictures of her from our running around days together when we were in our thirties. I took pictures of those photos with my iPhone so I could have them with me. I did that in 2017 after she appeared in that galley and spelled out her name with puffs of white clouds against a blue sky; what a magical moment. And then after that, things really began to happen. It's amazing what spirits can do from the other side of the veil.

Chapter Eleven:

Village Condo

The year was 2018. But even a few years before 2018, I was traveling to Sedona, AZ to attend Barbara Marciniak's seminars where she channeled the Pleiadians. Sometimes I attended twice a year. But on this particular trip to Sedona in April of 2018 I had just spent about fifteen hundred dollars for fifteen days in a motel to attend back-to-back weekends of Barbara Marciniak's seminars. One day as I was sitting in the seminar, I noticed a Zillow text for a furnished place to rent nearby for a month, which would be cheaper than what I just paid for two weeks at a hotel. So I made an appointment to see the place and left the seminar early. I had no clue then, but in retrospect, I think perhaps Rosie was working some magic for me. Because I was confident and sure footed about seeing this place. When I got to the condo in the nearby village, the owner sized me up. I guess she had probably done a credit score check on me and decided to make me an offer.

"Instead of renting it for a month" she offered, "how

about two hundred dollars less per month if you rent it for a year?"

"Okay," I said, it sure did not take me long to make up my mind. I loved the view from the condo, and I had a great feeling there was something spiritual about what was happening; maybe Rosie helped me find this condo for a magical psychic reason.

Little did I know that I was on a psychic mediumship mission for Rosie, my guide who had reintroduced herself to me just the previous year in 2017 at the Julia Marie mediumship galley. Where Rosie so brilliantly introduced herself to me by spelling out her name in puffs of clouds against a blue sky up in my mind's eye in front of me as I sat in my chair. The spirit of my passed Rottweiler, Emma, was there too. Rosie and Emma came and sat to the left of my chair. Rosie had said, "You are the medium, I will bring them forward to you." And I would soon discover that Rosie placed me near the subject. Yes, they had me on a mission 1200 miles away moving from the Midwest to the Southwest. Oddly enough, this is how my Pleiadians friends work with me. Around 2005, I was leaving a relationship situation. In retrospect I realized that it was time for me to work with spirit and follow a different path rather than being a partner in a relationship.

At the time I was visiting a medium named Jeannine, and she would channel the spirit of Ezekiel. Ezekiel told me in so many words that I needed to move on with my life and be on my own. I would surprise myself, as I did not know where the words came from, I would find myself saying in stressful moments, "Well I can always move to Sedona." I had never been there, but my guides had me remember clearly what my aunt and uncle back in the mid-nineties said about how beautiful it was there. When I heard that and the word Sedona, it resonated with me, as if something that may come up in my future. Funny how my Pleiadian guides gave me hints of what was to come. I was becoming more mobile, more adventurous, as I was being guided by the Pleiadians and my guide Rosie.

In June of 2013, after I bought my Toyota Prius that came with GPS, I was not afraid of traveling on my own. It appeared I was beginning to develop more interest and expanding my psychic experience; I was leaning toward the mystic, psychic and mediumship path. I visited gem shows and the psychic fair in Raleigh, NC. And I attended Barbara Marciniak seminars at Dancing Moon bookstore while I was there. I had already read her Pleiadian books. She channels the Pleiadians, which caught my attention right at the beginning. I believed that I was led to her seminars and her books for a reason. And then coincidentally I learned that Barbara Marciniak also held seminars in Sedona, AZ. So I ventured to Sedona and for about four years straight, I attended her seminars there most times twice a year, Spring and Fall.

In the Spring of 2018, I attended one of Barbara Marciniak's seminar in Sedona, while there I had been staying at the Green Tree hotel for two weeks for $1700, when at lunch on the last day seminar, I noticed that

I had received a Zillow message on my iPhone. It just showed up big on the locked face of my iPhone. I got the feeling and I knew that my guide Rosie, put it there. I suddenly had the urge to check it out. It was about a condo in a nearby village, one bedroom, one bath, furnished for $1700 a month short term. I thought, instead of two weeks I can stay for a whole month for the same amount. Something drove me to make an appointment with the owner and go see it. When I was there, I guess she had already done a credit check on me, as she then said, for two hundred less per month, I would like to rent it to you for a year. I believe Rosie had me feel very sure about it, so in April of 2018, I said yes to signing the one-year lease. Little did I realize that not only had I signed a lease for a year, but that I had just signed up for a rather magical mediumship mission. So in my case, not only do I do mediumship readings in person or over Zoom, seems that I get put on psychic mediumship missions.

So yes, later on about a month later, I realized that I was on a psychic mediumship mission. In fact, later I would find out that I was living right across the street from the subject, the sitter. Rosie my wonderful guide and the Pleiadians found me housing directly across the street from the subject. The subject I soon discovered was an attractive woman about ten years younger than I and we kept running into each other. I kept running into her outside as we lived right across the street from each other. There was just something mystical and spiritual about her, and about how she made me feel.

At the time, I had just come from a Mavis Pittalla four-day mediumship seminar in Chicago in the Fall of 2017 and there was a medium there that was similar to the woman across the street. I even asked her one day if she had a sister in Chicago, that was a medium. When I was standing face to face with her, the subject, I felt a spirit to her left, a large presence. The presence was like sprinkled brown sugar floating in the air in my mind's eye, is the closest thing as to how I can describe it, but much less dense. A spirit was hanging around her. At the time if I had asked about a passed loved one she might had responded differently. But something kept me from asking her if she had lost a passed loved one. I could have said that I sensed male figure who had passed at a young age. Something held me back. I guess the timing was not right according to Rosie and the Pleiadians and the past spirit. Or perhaps the spirit himself, was not yet ready for me to know him. I was beginning to learn that spirit has a way of guiding the medium, in ways of what they ask, say, the timing of chance meeting, and the questions I ask. I am a mere conduit and spirit speaks through me. Evidently it was not quite the right time for the spirit at her side to come forward to the forefront of my questions. As time went on, there were many chance meetings at the mailbox or trash dumpster which at the time I did not realize that a certain spirit attached to her was planning those "chance" meetings. I began to feel her heartfelt energy. Whatever was going on was apparently clearly meant to be. I was on a mission, it was magical. Rosie had found the perfect place for me to live while I was on this mission. It never fails to amaze me just how magical working with spirit can be.

After a while I could feel her, the sitter's, energy become even more intense. It felt as if her energy expanded out in a radius of at leaset five hundred feet around her. It was intense. I could feel her energy in my heart like a Mavis Pittalla prayer. I began to feel her energy in my heart that way, even when she was not at home. It was powerful. It was like a soul to soul energy, I felt it in my heart, much like that intense heart feeling I felt when Mavis Pittalla said her prayers each day before we began our sessions at her seminar in Chicago. I felt that there was something spiritually special about the woman from across the way. I felt her in my heart. When I spoke with her, I continued to feel a large spiritual presence near her. As she and I got to know each other and spoke more and more when we happened to see each other outside, I sensed that the spirit was always with her. I connected that strong feeling I got with the Chicago seminar, especially a woman there who looked a bit like my neighbor, but I felt there was a clearer presence, a strong presence, a more insistent presence staying around her, someone was hanging around her. I wondered if she felt it too. I was beginning to think maybe there was a connection somehow. So I asked, but she said she did not know anyone in Chicago and I left it go at that with the questions, thinking maybe the timing was not quite right yet.

Later on down the road, I had come to realize that her

passed over cousin, Steve, was probably arranging all of these chance meetings, so we would get to know each other. He had plans to use me because I am a medium. At one point back in around 2005, when I was studying mediumship and the Pleiadians, I did open myself up to be a medium for past over souls on the other side of the veil. I offered to help only the good spirits, to help them to connect with their living loved ones still in the physical. But only the good spirits, I insisted. And by galactic spiritual rule spirits have to honor that wish. Only the good spirits are to come forward for my mediumship readings and my help.

I kept having chance meetings with my neighbor across the street, and I was beginning to feel a real soul connection with her. I was beginning to feel that I was on a mission for a spirit and that I would soon learn the details. We saw each other more and more and she and I became friends after that first year I moved to another condo. More about that later. From time to time, she and her husband would go back east. I was always sorry to see her leave town for a while as she and her husband headed out of town to go back east, for about a month, each time. And when she was out of town she and I stayed connected. We continued to communicate via email, text and phone conversations. One day we were communicating with emails, and we were speaking of sad or tragic moments in our lives that we had to go through. She told me that when she was about twelve years old and her cousin was fifteen years old that he tragically died in an auto accident. Bingo! As soon as I read that I thought that was him, the spirit I kept seeing to her left, when I faced her and talked with her. In a way, I was surprised that I did not ask her on those times, if she lost a loved one. Popular TV medium Teresa Caputo sure does. I love her TV show and reel clips on Facebook where she does random readings.

Yes, as soon as I read what my neighbor wrote about her cousin passing in 1969 at age 15, I realized what my mission was to consist of. I felt his presence near me even more so then. He was right to the right of me. I could feel him with me most of the time. So soon I began to connect the dots and I realized my guides had me on a serious mission, I mean come on, they even found me housing, twice. The next day while coming back from a hike, either he or my guide Rosie put the thought in my head to ask the spirit what shall I call you. Immediately I saw white puffs of clouds, spelling out the name, Steve. And then I heard, "Not Steven."

I was so thrilled. I felt very connected to him. I knew right then and there that I was on a mission and that is why my guide Rosie found me housing right across the street from the subject/sitter of all places. It amazes me how spirit can work such magic. I love being connected with spirit.

Just a year or so prior, in Julia Marie's intuition mediumship reading gallery, the spirit of Rosie, now my guide, had reintroduced herself to me by spelling out her name with a puffs of white clouds against a blue sky background, and that was when she told me something I loved hearing.

"You are the medium," Rosie said, "I will bring them forward to you." So, my guides and the Pleiadians had me on a path that began when I was a kid to prime me for later own to study psychology, Astrology and then to study mediation, intuition, and mediumship. I was merely allowing things to happen step by step, I did not have a serious plan in mind to become a medium. I just thought I had intuition and lots of good common sense.

About two years later, from when I moved across the street from the sitter and met her cousin in spirit, Steve, I recalled Rosie telling me that I was a medium and she would bring them forward. And I remembered her saying that when I would feel my neighbor's cousin's spirit all around me. In early 2019 about a year later, when my lease was about up at the first place and much to my appreciation because the subject/sitter's spiritual energy was so strong, I wondered if I could move just a little further way from her.

I was at a physic mediumship meeting in Sedona I thought to ask Rosie for guidance.

"Rosie, shall I rent the next place I see in this complex," I asked.

"Yes, yes, yes," she said. In my mind's eye I saw floating words of "yes," all over the place. I felt so fortunate as the very next day I received my new home gift.

Rosie and the Pleiadians had found me another place to rent right around the corner from the previous place, only larger a two bedroom, two bath condo, but unfurnished, so it was cheaper than the first one bedroom furnished place. My first condo which was directly like fifty feet across from the subject's condo, lease was due up in a couple of months but little to my knowledge, until much later when I connected the dots of events, I came to realize that I was miraculously being guided.

The experience was so magical. See what spirit can do from the other side of the veil. Amazingly, the very next day, I walked over to the bank of mailboxes to check my mail. And something, actually Rosie, I realized later on, had me feel like walking a little way down that street. And miraculously, within a few steps I saw a for rent sign. And it was exactly the place where my best friend from St. Louis who was visiting earlier that year as she and I were walking the grounds one day around the complex she said.

"Down there is where you want to live," my best friend said pointing to a roll of condos adjacent to the golf course. I was thrilled to see the for rent sign and immediately felt my St. Louis friend's connection with the Pleiadians. She was speaking for them, and I felt it that day she said that while we were walking. She has her Sun and a couple of other planets in the sign of Taurus so she too is from the Pleiades. I only have the north node of the moon in Taurus. You are from the Pleiades if in your Astrology natal birth chart you have any asteroid, Sun, Moon, planet or south or north node of the Moon in the sign of Taurus in your natal birth chart. And that means that you are from the Pleiades. By the way come to find out that the subject/sitter across the street from the first place I rented has her Sun and a couple of other planets in the natal birth chart in the sign of Taurus. So she is from the Pleiades also. When I spotted the For Rent sign I immediately called the rental office phone number on the sign. It all was so magical, I was thrilled.

"We are about to close for the day," the receptionist said when I called. "Come in on Monday morning and get the key to look it over," she said.

Needless to say, I was anxious all weekend; but, in my heart I felt I might get the place, even when I heard other people were interested in it. So, I was there at the rental office at eight that morning as soon as they opened. I got the key and checked the unit out. It was untouched since the 1980's and reminded of the appliances I had in the first nice apartment I rented in the 1980's. It was fine with me, that the condo I was looking at was not updated and unfurnished, and the rent was cheaper. So Perfect!. I love original one-time owner retro 1980's fixtures. I told my best friend, and she said go for it, and I signed the lease. Although it was unfurnished it was two-bedrooms, two-baths--so nice for my friends to come visit.

My best friend was excited and advised, "Just buy some cheap furniture.

"Sounds like a good idea," I said. I always considered her advice as I knew and felt that the Pleiadians spoke through her.

"Thank you, Rosie and the Pleiadians and thanks for my best friend giving me that hint as to what was to come when she and I took that walk that day," I remember feeling magical when she said "down there is where you want to live." I think it is amazing how they, my guide Rosie and the Pleiadians give me hints and clues. So I have learned to pay attention and to just learn to be open to receiving those messages that come in positive feeling messages. And I have learned to separate those messages from my own thoughts. I was so grateful and I thank Rosie and the Pleiadians every day for this gift and the gift of being on a obvious psychic mediumship mission. I figured Rosie really wanted me there as she found me housing, twice now. I felt so gifted, but more was to come.

Rosie actually left me a gift that I found the day I moved into that second condo. There was an eagle feather lying parallel to my back patio on the grass. I graciously retrieved it and I have it lying with some other treasured items on the shelf of my television stand. It is so magical to have my guides and the Pleiadians to guide me. I suspect Rosie is a Pleiadian too, as my best friend is and the subject/sitter Steve's cousin is across the way.

The energy of the new place felt great, peaceful and calm. I could feel the Sedona red rock vortex even better there. My neighbor's energy back across the way, opposite the other condo, was so strong, even when she was not at home I felt it, it was almost too intense, and that is why I was happy to move five hundred feet across the way where I felt it less intense but still felt her wonderful spiritual energy.

I think Rosie made the second condo feel magical to me. Everyday, when I look at the eagle feather and see the beautiful view from my patio door I say. "Thank you, Rosie,"

I say words of appreciation every day for my Pleiadian family and Rosie for keeping me "healthy, wealthy and wise and safe from injury" which is my short prayer I say throughout the day. I know they keep me safe. It is their plan for me to stay out of the for-profit, poor health allopathic medical system aimed to keep you coming back suffering pill and jab side effects.That is the way it is designed because our good health would not make them any money. I realize it is an unsafe chemical based medical system and I am most grateful to know to eat only organic and pray that big Pharma and chemical do not destroy all that is organic, as I feel that reptiles are behind the illuminati and that their puppet slaves in power are the reptilian humanoid hybrids in powerful positions that David Icke writes about in his many books. I love to learn, and I know that my Pleiadian guides have me on a particular mission.

I love to learn, especially these days since the c19 debacle began. When I am not reading or writing I love to get outdoors in the sunshine and go for a hike. I recall often that magical day when I was out for a hike just thinking about my neighbor and how she told me about her cousin who passed away tragically at such a young age in an auto accident. On the way back home, I was still thinking about him. And I recall how he put the thought into my head, or Rosie did, to ask him that question.

"What do I call you?" I had asked. My mediumship instructor always said, ask what do I call you, instead of saying what is your name, something having to do about them living multiple life times and having multiple names.

I reflect often on that magical day, when I saw the name Steve spelled out in puffs of white clouds against a blue sky just the same way that Rosie spelled out her name, with puffs of white clouds against a blue-sky background. And "not Steven" I heard. That day Steve had proceeded to give me lots of clues about himself and what he liked to wear and do. And this goes back to 1969.

I was excited; I had messages to give my neighbor, but she was out of town. I could sense that Steve was excited to reconnect with his beloved cousin. They were very close, much more like brother and sister than cousins I sensed. I saw many items of evidence to share with his cousin, the sitter. He was fifteen years old when he passed in 1969, so I had clairvoyant visions of the shoes he liked, such as loafers and buckskin boots, khaki pants with pleats in the front and a silver bucket like loop on the back waistband. I envision him wearing a tennis sweater across his shoulders and the sleeves tied together in the front. I saw baseball cards with baseball players wearing those wool uniforms they wore back then. He loved playing baseball and collecting and trading baseball cards. He loves his cousin very much and watches out over her, like he did when he was fifteen and she twelve. He continues to watch over her. When I got back home, I wondered how I could get her over to my place so Steve could reconnect with her.

"She just got back from out of town," I told Steve telepathically, "you will have to help me get her over here," And then I heard telepathically.

"Watch this," Steve said, which made me smile. See I swear spirits from the other side can work magic. Just as Steve had her and I always running into each other when out for a walk, getting the mail or going to the trash. She and I became friends and had begun riding our bikes, walking and hiking together. I believe I felt in my heart his love for her. It is a soul love and I believe that it is eternal.

I was not totally surprised when within thirty minutes, I got a text from her.

"What are you doing?" she asked. "Can I come over." It was raining, and she ran over with her umbrella I was then across the way five hundred feet away instead of fifty feet away from her place.

When she got to my place, she was all talkative, I stood in the kitchen, she on the other side of the snack bar sitting on a stool. I felt Steve's presence over my left shoulder. A huge presence. I felt his energy. He was so excited and so impatient. "Tell her, tell her, I'm here." I heard.

She talked about this and that, we had not seen each other for a while as she was out of town. I felt Steve's impatience, "tell her that I am here" he repeated. I telepathically told him, that "I am trying, I need to wait for a low in the conversation. Finally she stopped to take a breath. I saw my chance and quickly interjected.

"Yes, I was going over that email recently, the one where you told me about your cousin 'Steve's' passing," I quickly interjected to see if she noticed that I somehow knew his name. She looked at me strangely as if she were trying to figure out if she told me his name or not. I had the email all printed out. She did not tell me his name.

"Steve told me his name himself when I was out for a hike yesterday," The moment was intense and I added,

"I have to sit down now," I said, as I walked right through Steve's spirit in the kitchen doorway to go sit down in my recliner. She moved to the other recliner. Steve was there in the room with us, but his presence was less intense or so it seemed to me, but I was busy thinking of all the items of evidence he had shared with me the day before. So I told her the evidence that he gave me. I added that he protects her and loves her more like a sister than a cousin. She concurred and verified all of it as she smiled then got up and moved over to the patio door to watch the rain pouring down outside. She had just arrived at my place before a heavy thunderstorm moved in.

"It's raining so hard," she said, "I might have to stay all night."

"That would be just fine," I said, and I meant it as I felt his love for her and it warmed my heart. I would have loved the company we could have talked and visited for hours. I had never fell in love with a mediumship sitter before in my life, but we were so much alike. Her Astrological natal birth chart sun is in Taurus, so she is a fellow Pleiadian starseed, so we are soul sisters in a way, as we are both starseeds from the Pleiades.

That evening after Steve's cousin left to go home, I was sitting up on my bed watching Open Minds with Regina Meredith on GAIA. Suddenly, I felt as if I had company. I got the feeling that Steve and Rosie enjoyed the mediumship visit with Steve's cousin so much that they wanted to come and visit me. I felt their happy energy enter my bedroom. Suddenly sitting next to me on the bed was my guide Rosie, she had on her jeans and a horizontal striped t-shirt she often wore when we were in our thirties. Next to her I felt another person, it was Steve. I can't quite see his face, because I have never met him in person. But, I am getting a better idea of a handsome man, tall and slender and he liked to wear khaki and crème colors. It seemed so real, that I felt that I had to scoot over closer to the edge of the bed to give Rosie and Steve more room. Emma was at the foot of the bed. It was quite a wonderful experience. I actually felt their presence. It was magical and priceless. They were happy, their spiritual energy was invigorating. They stayed for what seems quite a long while watching GAIA TV with me. It is a magical spiritual moment that I will never forget. I was happy to know that they were pleased with the mediumship reading with Steve's cousin. I am sure that Steve watches over his cousin and guides her and I have a feeling she connects with him too and feels his loving protective presence all around her.

So now along with Rosie, Emma and the Pleiadians, I feel Steve's presence with me all the time. He is my guide now too, as I am sure he watches over and protects his beloved cousin. A fun thing happened a few weeks later.

Steve's cousin and I were uptown shopping, she saw a small iPhone holder type purse that she liked. She could not decide if she wanted to buy it or not, so she hung it behind two other purses on the rack in a way to safely hide it in case she wanted to come back and get it. Watching her do that warmed my heart. What woman has not done that, hide an item behind two other items on the rank, just in case we decide to come back and get it. And her doing that confirmed that no matter where we grow up in the country, women are basically all the same. I have done it myself, I know that I have, and most every woman I know has hung the purse behind two other or move purses to secure it safety hidden from other shoppers, and hopefully hide their new found treasure so no one else buys it before they decide if they really want it. On the way home, she had second thoughts about the purse. She pondered as I drove us towards home.

"Maybe I should have gotten the purse," she said.

"I can turn around and go back," I said, "I don't mind, if you would like to go back and get it."

"No, that's okay," she insisted.

As soon as I dropped her off and got home. I got a

strong telepathic message from Steve to go back and get the purse for her. The moment I got the idea and urge to do that, I knew the idea to go back get the purse was from Steve and probably Rosie too. I knew that if I went to get the purse for her, that he would have traffic cleared the whole six miles or more I had to drive; that I would find parking very easily and convenient to the store and that the purse would still be there, right where she hung it, behind the other two. And so it went just like that, there was no traffic at all and usually there is a backup when getting closer to the shopping area, but not today. I found close parking. And I walked straight inside the store and back to where the purses were hung and found that the purse was still hanging behind the other two, right where I saw her hang it. And to top it all off, when I took it off the rack and turned around, I saw that the clerk was standing at the register and was watching and waiting for me, and ready to check me out. Talk about magical and spiritual events. Spirits rock!

I love this stuff. I was flying high. I was back home with her gift within thirty minutes. I couldn't wait to tell her the story how Steve had put the idea in my head, and since I knew that he did, I knew traffic would be light and the parking easy and that the purse would be right where she hung it. I was thrilled to tell her the story and that the purse was a gift from her cousin Steve. She and Steve both remain in my heart. She has since moved back east but her spirit and his spirit will forever be with me. So apparently my psychic medium path and journey have more magical moments to come. As Steve remains my guide.

I was missing his cousin after she moved away. She had been my muse as I published two books in three years while she lived near me because I felt her energy. It's been a couple of months, and I had really been feeling her in my heart. So I asked Steve for help. I usually go to an open mic on Monday evenings but on this particular day I just was not into it, could not talk myself into gathering my things and going. A few minutes after I normally leave to go to it, I think Steve had me feel it was a good time to text his cousin. In a few minutes she texted back. It was great as we swapped texts and got caught up. I was feeling pretty down, missing her and I think Steve helped with the timing, which was a good time for her too, so I would text her. I am sure he contributed to my feelings for her, as I may be feeling his love for her. I think he wants to keep her and I connected too. I told him, that in the beginning I was the medium to connect him and her.

And now since she moved away, I told Steve that he is the medium to keep us connected. As we texted back and forth, she sounded like she was doing good so I was happy for her. I told her about having the base player and the percussion guy accompany me as I sang "Big Boss Man" and played my ukulele on open mic night. I told her that it was such a treat to have accompanying base and percussion player. We got compliments too I said. She and I both shared what was going on with us. It was just what I needed short of being able to see her in person. I miss having her living close by, but at least I got to talk to her. It did me a world of good. I thanked Steve profusely for helping to arrange it and giving me the strong urge to text her when I did, I caught on later on that he wanted me to stay home probably the time was perfect for her for us to get together.

See how my guides help me out. Rosie does the same thing and I know Emma with her rose in her mouth for me, my Rottweiler, protects me. Everyday I hug my little Emma puppy when I make the bed and her tittle buddy Frenchie, too. Her little buddy is a French bulldog I got for her to keep her company, they both sit on the bed pillows and "guard the house" while I am gone running errands or hiking or biking.

Chapter Twelve:

Village Ukulele

I received another magical gift from the Pleiadians when I rented the first place back in the Spring of 2018, that was across from the sitter. The place was furnished and as I was carrying some things into the condo. I noticed a local weekly news, activity, and entertainment paper laying on the counter. It's a paper that listed activities and musical events. Right on the front cover of the paper my attention was drawn to a group of people. As I looked closer I saw it is a ukulele group that meets each week right down the street from where I was staying. And I just happened to have my ukulele with me.

Just how far back does the planning begin? I wondered. I can remember when I would get depressed even talking to someone, I found myself saying "will I guess I can always go to Arizona." Actually, I surprised myself and thought now where did that come from. I think from my guides and Pleiadians were speaking through me. The first hint I guess was that the idea got planted even back in the late 1990's when I heard my aunt and uncle returning from the northern Arizona vacation say Sedona area and Grand Canyon was so beautiful. There was something about hearing them say that, that intuitively struck a chord with me. I was to hear that for a reason, and it was to resonate with me for a reason.

See how far back the spiritual mystical journey plannings can begin? Like why did I switch from playing the guitar to playing the ukulele? I guess so I could join that group and get to know people, and preform on open mic night. Something I had always wanted to try to do. I love open mic because it is the great common denominator, as no matter man or woman we are all nervous to do open mic. It's been three years now since performing open mic for sure two or three times a month.

So, I am getting better at not being nervous. It is great, I feel, to push the envelope once in a while and test your nerves. At home when I practice and video myself and listen back. If I think I sound good enough that day, I'll upload the video to the feed and reels on Facebook. So that's keeps me practicing.

I get a kick out of asking the archangels to help out the nervous performers at open mic. This one woman plays the violin. It must take all she has to get up there in front of people and play. I have seen her take her name off the list after being fifth or lower on the list. If she is like me the longer you have to wait the more nervous you become. On one particular evening, she kept her name on the list and got up there in front of us to play her violin. She hesitated to take and breath.

"I don't know how anyone can get up here and do this, I'm a wreck," she gasped.

When I heard her say that, I summoned the archangels.

"Would you archangels please help her out, help her be calm. And have her sound really good."

She had three songs to do. Her first was a little rocky, not really bad. Toward the end of the first song, I saw wings, full to the floor white thick angel wings showing out from behind her back, on either side of her. Her second song was very good, her third song was excellent, and it was as if she did not even want to quit playing. She did good. I gave her the thumbs up as she smiled at folks who told her she did great. I didn't tell her of course, that's half the fun so she knew that she did it all on her own. That was so fun to do that for her. People, keep that in mind, you can help people every day like that.

I get a lot of views on my singing and playing ukulele Facebook reels. I mention them on DianneTheMedium. com and on *DianneTheMedium* podcast on PodBean. So take a listen.

Sometimes I wonder just how far back in time were these plans to get me to the position where I end a twenty-year living together relationship that I believe was a spiritual mission that I was on for my best friend's parents. And now that they are both passed, I ask them to please watch out over her and please keep her safe, healthy, wealthy and wise and going organic. I don't really trust our modern day allopathic for-profit medical system. We humans are organic and spiritual.

When my best friend's mother passed while at the funeral home visiting with all the relatives, I saw her mother standing near the head of her coffin. She was standing holding the chalice and host offering like she and her husband did in church every Sunday morning. I tried to tell family members what I saw, but I believe spirit thought I rather not do that. Because it seems so obvious, it was like I was invisible with each small group I approached and I could not interject or get a word in edgewise, so I just gave up and thought that it was not meant to be.

The same thing happened a few years later when her father passed. At the funeral home, I saw them both this time standing near the head of his coffin. He had the wine chalice, and she had the host plate as if they were ready to pass out communism during a mass. Again I tried to interject and mingle with small groups. Apparently it was not meant for me to get people's attention to tell them what I saw. Again it was like I was invisible. So once again I figured it was not meant to be.

I love the way I connect with and see spirit. Mostly when I listen to psychic mediums speak on various GAIA TV shows, the mediums are not on missions, that they talk about anyway. But I plainly have my spirit guides Rosie and the Pleiadians for sure helping me. They found housing for me, twice, for this one mission. I truly feel blessed and honored to be representing the Alycone Pleiadians here on Earth. And what an honor to have them tell me that I am from Alcyone of the Pleiades. That mission was more recent of course;

but back around 2011 or so, I experienced a medical intuition and psychic reading. With a member of our walk-run group. Spirit power is amazing to me, and I love how they just suddenly show up and show me things in my mind's eye clairvoyantly.

Chapter Thirteen:

Sensing Breast Cancer

It was after a run, and we all gathered at a restaurant to celebrate and send off a member who was heading to England to participate in a marathon run event there. We all shared a long table. I sat across from my friend. We were in the middle of a conversation comparing various brands of running shoes when I suddenly sensed and felt that my friend who was currently speaking to me had breast cancer in her right breast. I pushed the thought and vision out of my mind as I continued to listen to her talk about running shoe prices and where to find good deals. Before long the vision came back again, I pushed it away again, wondering why I was sensing and seeing the imagine. But the message was relentless. I also sensed then that she being a medical professional was trained enough and would see the rash or feel a discomfort and become concerned enough to visit her doctor. So I did not say anything right then. My plan was to wait a day or so before I returned to the issue, although I was concerned.

After all, who walks up to someone and says, "I think you need your right breast checked out I am sensing a cancer." I was concerned. But they moved things on quickly enough as my friend informed me of her partner's suspicions soon after. So I knew she was taking care of it. So I never had to say what I sensed. As in a day or two her partner in passing just happened to let me know that she saw a rash and felt that something was wrong and went to see the doctor and they were beginning treatment the next day or so. So, clearly, getting in touch with your spiritual and psychic guides and being in tuned and working with them can be very rewarding and it can be magical.

Chapter Fourteen:

Zoom Toronto

Remember Rosie said back in 2017, "You are the medium, I will bring them forward." Well she has. One most rememberable reading was a notice I got from my DianneTheMedium.com web site. I received an email from my contact page and she said, "Something drew me to your website." My guide Rosie came immediately to mind. I knew she drew the young woman from Toronto to my site. I got back with her via her email and we set up a day and time to do the reading over Zoom.

The day came, I saw a lovely young woman. In the email I told her to allow about an hour and do not say or tell me anything about who or what you want to come through. I am a mere conduit. I told her I close my eyes lean a little inward toward the sitter's left. I push my own thoughts to the side, and I am like an open conduit ready to receive. I wait and then usually in a couple of seconds I sense and clairvoyantly see an imagine. With this young woman I saw a father figure, like a grandfather. I got that she took care of him before he passed. I sensed that she was nearing the age if you are going to have a baby its best to have it now.

From the grandfather I got, "this is the twenty-first century, if you have the means and if you want to have that little girl, you go right ahead and have her." Then I saw, and I believe her grandfather helped with the imagine, that I saw. I saw her and her little girl about two or three years old, both with long dark hair. The little girl sitting next to her, was a spitting image of her mother. Just adorable. It made me cry. And she cried too when I opened my eyes and told her what I got. It was beautiful and magical, and I am sure she had that little girl. See how wonderfully miraculously connecting with the other side of the veil can be?

Chapter Fifteen:

c19 Escape

Ever since I bought a 2013 Toyota Prius with GPS, I hit the road solo; the GPS gave me that much confidence. I did not have to worry about getting lost. I use it a lot on short trips just to know when my exit is coming up. I made many road trips to the Southwest then to Barbara Marciniak's Pleiadian seminars. She channeled the Pleiadians. I was in the Southwest late in 2019 when covid came about and the jab mandate. People were being shamed by the media to get the jab are responsible for killing their neighbor by spreading the virus. My dad would have been proud of me, for I did not jump off the bridge with the rest of them. Truth be told, they would have had to drag me kicking and screaming to get that jab especially since it was a free jab offered from a very for-profit minded medical and drug industry. Remember I am a psychic medium, so why would I trust the jab, when I do not trust the pills, nor the genetically modified organisms created as pretend food.

It is very plain to see that yes, unscrupulous reptilian humanoid hybrids males have positioned themselves into powerful positions. They are greedy and can easily be won over and persuaded with money. I have a lack of trust in the system. Of course, patients who went regularly for their wellness visits of course, had their doctors push hard for them to get the jab. I realize that a doctor makes their money only by pushing doctor visits, meds and procedures. I was fortunate that my guides were very clear: No jabs. I merely made sure that I ate organically, researched and took the best supplements to keep my immune system built up. I believe only we can keep ourselves healthy by keeping our immune systems strong and without injecting or swallowing medicines that are chemical.

We humans are not chemical, but made up of vitamins and minerals. I spent much of my time in the lovely Southwest, hiking and getting plenty of healthy sunshine. Vitamin D is so important for getting cholesterol to our brains and its helps your DNA so I read. So I was fortunate to be out and about while the manipulated, mandated world rolled up their sleeves and stood obediently in line, only afterward to feel like crap and to learn that many suffered bad jab side effects.

For many years already, my Pleiadian family and guides had me ease away from modern allopathic medicine pills and jabs. They did not want foreign chemicals in my body, as the human body is made up as is all of nature of vitamins and minerals. I was guided rather to foraging and natural home remedies. As I listened to spirit.

Chapter Sixteen:

The Spirit of Edie

The year was 2009, I believe that my Pleiadian guides and my guide Rosie, who had not reintroduced herself to me yet as that happened in 2017. But nevertheless, she was with me in spirit. I had no idea that I was a psychic medium. I was living with my partner at the time we had moved from the log home back into my Belleville, IL condo. At the time I was regularly visiting Jeannine, a psychic median who channeled the spirit of Ezekiel.

I also joined a run/walk group that met in Forest Park in St. Louis three times a week. The ladies always talked about a woman named Marcia who was a great marathoner, and they were so amazed that she completed the Ironman event. If you are not familiar with it, an Ironman event is an all-day event. Well, it would take me a week, I am sure. I am not sure of the order of events, but an Ironman consists of running a full marathon that is 26.2 miles, then biking 100 miles and then swimming about 2 miles, I think it is. All in one day. She completed it! And as most participants do then, she got the Ironman tattoo on the calf of her leg. She definitely deserved bragging rights. I can't even imagine. I have ran many half-marathons and that was enough. I have ridden my bike a hundred miles in one day, several times over the years, I can't imagine doing anything else in the same day after I competed either a half marathon or a century. .

Marcia and I got to know each other and began hanging out, boy did I ever get a workout, trying to keep up biking and running with her. When I did centuries on my bike, I would ride fifty miles in one direction and then turn around and ride back fifty miles. As time went on, I did four loops of twenty-five miles each near my parked car in a large park. I ran several half marathons a year. In retrospect, I think the heavy hard running and biking work outs helped with my Post Traumatic Stress Symptom left over from my childhood. I think the Pleiadians and my guides had me train and condition myself, for my mental and physical health, and so I could hang out and keep up with Marcia when the time came. Of course I could only see that in retrospect years later. I had come to realize that all my training was all a warmup for the main event, and that was to get to know her so I could eventually get her to go to my psychic Jeannine who channeled Ezekiel. I was beginning to catch on that perhaps Edie was working through me, even speaking through me which I only came to figure out much later.

Marcia and I would usually meet up at my condo. I

began to notice that on most visits she would some how manage to talk about Edie, her good friend who was a commercial artist. Marcia had modeled for her from time to time. Edie had passed about a year or so before and Marcia did the memorial for her. I began saying things about Edie that just popped out of my mouth, as if I was a channel and someone was speaking through me. It was surprising to me, like, where did that come from.

"I think Edie watches over you," I found myself saying one day when she spoke of Edie as she usually did. Always somehow Edie got into the conversation, so it seemed.

"Oh, that Edie," Marcia said when I said that.

One day when Marcia came over to my place, she brought a box of pictures and awards that Edie had gotten through the years for her artistry work. I bet Edie had her do that! I looked through the box with her.

"Oh, my Edie looks the same at age eighty as she did was she was in the service," I found myself saying. I meant it, but I began to think that the spirit Edie was putting words in my mouth. Because suddenly there was a flash thought to okay it and then the words just came out, without me actually thinking of them. So I know that the spirit of Edie was speaking through me.

"I think Edie would like to speak to you," I found myself saying on the next visit when Marcia came over for a bike ride.

"Oh, that Edie," smiled Marcia, "wait, what?"

That one threw her off, you see Edie knew that I

regularly visited Jeannine the psychic medium who channeled Ezekiel, at least twice a year I had been going. The more I reflect back on it, I think the Pleiadians and my guides had me go to Jeannine. I believe that they had me leave a relationship so I could get on with my psychic mediumship work that the guides and the Pleiadians had planned out for me, all of this unknown to me, of course. So the living-together ended, and we remain good friends to this day; but, eventually perhaps we both had special paths to be on.

Marcia did not believe in psychic woo woo stuff as she referred to it. I had some convincing to do, but I was catching on and believed that Edie would help me get Marcia to an appointment with Jeannine the psychic medium who channeled the spirit of Ezekiel.

After I had brought it up on several occasions, Marcia finally agreed to an appointment for a reading with Jeannine. So I called her. Usually she is pretty booked up and I usually know that it may be a few weeks before I can get a reading. So, I called to make the appointment while Marcia was at my place. To my surprise Jeannine just happened to have a cancellation for the next day, and luck, or was it, would have it that Marcia was off the next day from her water aerobics teaching job at the YMCA. So we were all set.

It was a lovely drive out to west county where Jeannine lived in an old English style historical home. The home was adorned with lace curtains and the whole turn of the century architecture and decor. While Marcia went back into the parlor with Jeannine, I sat in the remodeled modern style kitchen which was to my distaste. Why on earth would you not remodel the kitchen cabinets and such to match the rest of the house. really, blonde kitchen cabinets? It kept me distracted even while I toiled to make conversation with her, bordering on Alzheimer's, husband. Finally, the hour was up and Marcia and Jeannine reappeared back in the out-of-place modern style, and the blonde cabinets were everywhere, kitchen. So unsettling to a libra who loves all things in balance and harmony.

I did not have a tape player in my car so we listened to the tape when we got back to my place. It was amazing. Routinely Ezekiel will blast you about yourself at the beginning of the reading. Like he did with Marcia as he suggested she decide rather she wants to be with a woman or her husband, like make up your mind, as you are not doing yourself or any one else any favors. Then Ezekiel asked Marcia a question.

"Is there someone who you wish to speak to?" he asked, "as there is a spirit anxiously awaiting to speak with you, pacing back and forth behind your chair."

"Edie," Marcia asked. The connection was made. Ezekiel was then to be the interpreter between Edie and Marcia.

Edie went on as saying to Marcia that she was sorry that she could not hang on any longer, as the cancer was too painful. She thanked Marcia for the beautiful memorial she gave for her when she passed. Then Marcia asked Edie a question. Ezekiel continued to be the channel, the interpreter between Marcia and Edie.

"Is Georgette there with you?" Marcia asked. Georgette, was Edie's partner for over thirty years. Toward the later years before Georgette got sick and passed, Marcia was modeling for Edie. And Marcia and Edie had an affair of which they thought Georgette did not know about, but evidently she did. And it probably did not do her health any good knowing it. So evidently Georgette who had already passed over was not there to welcome Edie when she passed over a year or so later. Not there, you know like everyone says that your passed loved ones will be there to greet you when you cross over.

So my summation was that Georgette knew of the affair and was not happy about it. See how your life story can continue on after you pass over? Nothing really changes when you pass, only your body dies, your spirit, your soul, your story, your personality remains the same.

"No, Georgette is not here with me, "Edie sadly said, "and I miss her."

"What is Georgette's last name," Ezekiel asked Marcia, and she told him.

"Oh, she comes quickly now," said Ezekiel. And then he proceeded to tell Marcia what he was seeing.

"Oh, they hug and blend together. Edie asked Georgette where have you been, and Georgette says to a beautiful place I call Jamaica."

So, listening to the tape, I got it. The spirits on the other side of the veil work through me to connect with another. I think it is why my Pleiadian guides, even way before I knew I was from Alcyone of the Pleiades, had me working for them. It is why I had to leave a relationship, it is why I joined the run walk group. Yes, they geared me up for this particular mission, long even before I was on it. See how spirit does. They gave me the idea to train to bike a hundred miles in one day, and the idea and desire to run half marathons, thankfully, I never had the desire to run a full marathon. Guess my guides thought a half marathon would be enough to get me in with the running group and to befriend Marcia.

Yes, I believe it is all planned ahead of time from the other side. Edie needed me, someone who just happened to go to Jeannine, a psychic. I guess they had planted that idea in my head too. Get it? See how spirits can work from the other side of the veil. They planned things, events, desires, people in my life, to work towards a particular mission. They know I only work with good spirits and they have to honor that. So my purpose as Edie, a passed over soul, planned it, was to have me befriend Marcia and to get Marcia to Jeannine so Edie could come through and together with Marcia's help apologize to Georgette so Georgette and Edie could then reunite on the other side. Get it?

Pretty amazing isn't it. I think it is magical. We have all this help from the other side and vice versa. I remember thinking right before all this went on probably after one of my visits to Jeannine, that if crossed over spirits can help us, why can't we help them if they need help. Wonder who planted that thought in my head?

Anyway, it got me on my Marcia and Edie adventure.

So the Pleiadians and guides had been using me I think too when I lived with my best friend for those years, that was a mission perhaps her guides and mine came up with, to help each other grow on our paths even as gay people. Their is no judgement on the other side of the veil, if there is, we souls to it to ourselves, and we judge ourselves according to the beliefs were learned while on Earth.

My guides always protected me on my adventures with Marcia as she pushed my physical limits when it came to running or biking. When we first started hanging out together, I had signed up for an over night bike ride trip from St. Charles, MO. A Katy Trail sixty-four mile bike ride to Herman, MO stay the night in a tent and then ride back the next day. There was a gag wagon that carried our tents and gear. Marcia is a Ironman athlete ---need I say more.

A couple weeks before the event, I figured I need to make a trial run from St. Charles to German in preparation. I geared up my bike. It was a tough ride of sixty-four miles. But riding on Katy Trail near German, I missed the exit, where I was supposed to get off the trail climb up the overpass embankment and ride along route 98 into Herman. Before I realized it, I rode on about fifteen more miles on the trail.

Finally, I came to a cross road. A man was turning onto it, he had a small child in the car and so he looked safe. He stopped and asked if I needed help. That was when I realized that I had missed the turnoff. He offered to somehow manage get my bike on the roof of his car and drive me back the fifteen miles to the exit point. I must have looked pretty tired. I thanked him profusely but told him I would just ride back.

"I hope that new bridge is in for you," he said. "They've been working on that bridge into Herman for a long time."

"New bridge," I said. A red flag went up in my mind. "You sure you don't want me to bungee your bike on my car," he asked again.

"My bike will scratch up the roof of your car." I said and politely refused and thanked him. He was really trying to help me. A good guy. I merely mustered up the strength, turned my bike around and rode back. When I got to the overpass, I climbed up the embankment and then rode my bike south along the shoulder of the road leading into German. When I got closer, I saw a new bridge was going in. I also saw that the old bridge into German was two lane and very minimal shoulder space. No lights either and it was getting to be close to the sun going down. I rode toward the new bridge alongside the old bridge.

That was when I saw the pickup truck driving towards me. I was in a construction area. I saw the driver had a woman with him that I figured was his girlfriend or wife, and that he was a worker there or a foreman checking out the work that was being done. So I felt safe talking to him. I asked if the bridge was all the way finished, that I was trying to ride my bike into Herman. He told me it was open across the river, so no it was not even near completion.

"How about you ride in front of me across the bridge," he said. I will hold back traffic for you. Since there really is no shoulder and no lights on the bridge."

This is when your Pleiadians send very nice men along the way to help you out. I was so grateful! If he would not have been there, I guess I would have gotten my tent off my bike and set it up at the new bridge site for the night. I cry when I thank my Pleiadians for sending that man. I pedaled like hell as I rode my bike as fast as I could in front of his truck and he creeped along behind me, his headlights lighting up my way. I doubt if I got up to sixteen miles an hour. As I had just ridden eighty miles.

But, this is where you learn that the power of mind over matter actually works. And if you really want to do something that you can. I pushed it. I was never so glad to get across the quarter mile span of bridge. As soon as I got across and there was a shoulder, I pulled over, waved and thanked him profusely. He sped up to the speed limit and a long trail of cars followed behind him. They saw just what the holdup had been all about as they saw me off to the side huffing and puffing trying to catch my breath.

I asked people where the park was, and they told me, just a few blocks along the Main Street, you'll see the sign. I found the turn off, it was getting dark and I wanted to get to the camp ground. As I biked along some softball diamonds in the park, women were playing softball.

Some idiot guy driving his car toward me was

watching them. I saw him gawking at them, not paying attention, as he was heading torward me. I was tired, and determined I was not going to take the dangerous rocky big sharp-edged stone-lined ditch, as there was no shoulder. The idiot in the car creeped along, gawking at the women, and about ready to run into me as he headed toward me. All I could do was stare at him, so I stared hard. I had no horn.

Finally my Pleiadians guides, I know it was them, woke the idiot up out of his crazed daze staring at the woman, and he finally looked my way and saw me and just in time jerk his steering wheel to the right to get back over to his side of the road. Whew, that was close.

Same thing happened to me one time when I went with the ladies to a trout fishing park. I was running facing the traffic, along a big ditch with only big huge rocks and no shoulder. I was as close to the rocks as I could get when some idiot driving a pickup truck was gawking at the fishermen to his left across the way. No, I was not going to take the ditch and bugger myself up. Finally, his wife, yelled at him and the driver looked my way and jerked his steering wheel to the left to avoid me.

See both times I would have injured myself with falling into the big rocks, so I know that my guides and the Pleiadians were helping me. I thanked them profusely. Its a dangerous world out there. So back in Herman I checked in at the camp ground and put my tent close to a family with two young kids, so it looked like I was part of their party. By this time, I was taking every precaution. I quietly put up my tent and crawled inside, ate something, got ready in lie down, and cover up. That was when the big frog in the creek behind my tent began his very loud croaking sounds, perfectly spaced out every ten seconds, like torture, all night long. I laid there managing to doze off and on until daylight and began my sixty-four mile trek back to St. Charles.

I rode my bike from Brentwood to St. Charles to begin my trek the day before. But this time, I called my friend who lives around the corner from me. She got my spare keys and drove my SUV with the bike rake on the back to Creve Coeur Park to pick me up. I was beat but I had a week to rest up, so I was ready for the weekend Herman ride with Marcia.

Thinking back I really pushed myself. I did a few more century rides, yes that's one hundred miles in one day. Since the 1980's I have done many of them, then I began running half marathons with the running group and doing less biking. One thing for sure, I stopped trying to keep up with Marcia.

Chapter Seventeen:

More Convenient Inconveniences

I have been very fortunate to have the Pleiadians and my guides with me on those bike trips and more recently, after I got my 2013 Toyota Prius with GPS, road trips. Of course, I always have my car regularly and properly maintained. I always took the mechanic's advice.

"You are going to need new tires soon," the mechanic said.

"Put them on today," I said. An ounce of precaution is priceless in the long run. My guides and Pleiadians help me but I need to help myself so they can help me. A treacherous weather driving experience comes to mind. Good thing I had new tires. I had my friend with me and my Pleiadians of course. I was driving south on 17 out of Flagstaff, AZ. It had begun to snow. I wasn't too worried as I was following the snowplow truck. That was going well, until he decided to pull off into the medium to help a disabled semi-truck. The snow as sticking, It was a white knuckle driving event for sure.

"Pleiadians, you are with me, right?" I asked as I grasped the steering wheel to not make any sudden moves. I stayed in the righthand lane. It's all downhill through there, which adding to the dangerous conditions. I was probably going thirty miles per hour. When a small pickup with a young male driver came up behind me. Soon, I saw where he was going to come around me. I knew he was asking for trouble, especially in a light pickup truck where the weight is in the front and very light over the back drive wheels. Well, he passed me. And then within a quarter mile, he went flying off into the medium. As I passed him, I saw that his truck had come to a halt, as he still sat there staring straight ahead with a frightful look on his face and both hands still holding tight on the steering wheel.

I proceeded cautiously and slowly, much to the appreciation of my friend who sat next to me.

"I'm just glad that you are driving, and not me," she said. She was keeping quiet so I could concentrate, I guess. And trust me I was concentrating not to make any sudden steering moves.

It wasn't too much longer, after the small light pickup truck slide off in to the medium when a BMW came up behind me. Yep you guessed it, another young white male. Seems I was going a little too slow for him on this snow packed highway. He came around me. A little way down the mountain side I saw him on the right side of the road in the ditch. Same as the other guy in the light pickup truck. This guy too, sat in his halted car, staring straight ahead with both hands still grasping the steering wheel. He had the same look on his face as the other guy did. My dad always taught me, hast makes waste.

The year before that, I had a snowy experience in Trinidad, CO. The roads were getting snowy as I was heading north to Denver. My friend called me on my cell phone and warned me that the roads would get worse heading to Denver.

"If I were you, I would take the next exit and head south back to New Mexico and not try to drive to Denver," she warned.

I have always believed that my Pleiadians spoke through her, as she has the Sun, and a few other planets in the sign of Taurus. So she is truly a Pleiadian. So, I listened and took the next exit. So, very typical of road crews, they cleared off the highway but not the overpasses themselves just the ramp leading up to them. I made it up to the overpass alright. And as I turned left to go across it. I saw that it was snow covered. I also spotted a semi at the west end of the overpass. The driver appeared to be have trouble backing up. Somehow he had gotten his rig, heading down the up ramp. So he was trying to back up to the flat part of the overpass, right where I was coming from.

I was driving a front wheel drive 2013 Prius. As I drove slowly across overpass, I felt the right front drive wheel slip, grab, then slip again. Then the drive power switched over to the left front drive wheel. It went like this back and forth, when the one wheel began to slip the drive power shifted to the other front wheel. But,

I kept slowly going. No way was I going to stop, for I knew I would sit and spin then and never get going again. So I crept along getting closer and closer to the rear of the semi which I saw backing up. I called for all the help I could get from my spiritual guides and my Pleiadian guides. The driver of the semi, once he had his rig moving was not going to stop, nor was I. My Pleiadians and guides all helped me as I kept moving trying to speed up just a little more.

It worked, thank you guides, as I just cleared the back end of that semi with about three feet to spare. And then immediately turned left down the ramp to head back to Santa Fe. As I drove to lower elevation, the snow turned to rain. Thank you guides. See, it helps to have friends in high places.

Trust me, I have never run, biked centuries in a day or traveled alone, ever. Your spirits guides and Pleiadian guides are wonderful and so is the human body; it is amazing, if you believe that it is and realize it, love it and respect it. For one thing physical activity and being outdoors is the best way to overcome depression or PTSD. Activity gets the oxygen flowing and up lifts your spirits. Plus just that idea of accomplishing something, a physical feat, automatically lifts your spirits. And it is a wonderful feeling to push yourself a bit and succeed at your endeavors. I have hiked long distances too in one day, like eleven or twelve miles. When I do any of the above I make sure I have water, and Bloc energy chews with electrolytes.

Of course, I have worked up to these events. Just

sitting here writing about it, makes me want to go for a three mile run around the neighborhood, as the sun is shinning. Might I advise everyone to get up get out and push your limits just a bit. Take it slow at first, and each time, add a little more distance or time to your workout. I think you will amazed.

I have been very blessed and have experienced my guides and the Pleiadians helping me to make my inconveniences a little more convenient. For example, when I worked off hours at the phone company, I got to park in the garage at work. A very convenient place when I discovered a flat tire. Nothing like having a flat tire in a lighted garage for the convenience of me and the AAA guy. But also what a blessing that if you are going to have a flat tire it doesn't end up happening on the road on my way home at midnight. Thank you guides.

I also appreciate in the newer car the low tire pressure indicator light in my later model 2016 Prius with low psi indicator and now GPS with radar detection so the cruise control automatically slows when you come upon a slow moving vehicle in front of you, put your left signal on when it's clear to move left, then if no one in front of you the cruise control, on its own, speeds and resumes to where you had it set.

Like I said, I liked the low psi indicator because one time it came on I had to add air, I mentioned it to my Toyota maintenance department manager. I told him which tire I had to add air to. They checked it out and they found a nail and fixed it. It's good to know these things and work together with your mechanics, guides and my Pleiadians.

Same thing when my car's twelve volt battery died. I was at home and the AAA guy jumped it and directed me to an O'Reilly's auto supply that was open. I was happy that it happened at home and the fix was convenient. Batteries die and you get another, bodies die, and our spiritual beings live on. Some people have near death experiences that change their lives. You don't have to flatline on the operating table. Just being near a death, and thinking you are next in line qualifies. I think I had one at nine years old.

Chapter Eighteen:

Near Death

Although I have never had a real near-death experience where I flat lined and was brought back, many say flat lining during surgery is not necessary for a near death experience. Just being near a death qualifies or thinking that your life is also being threatened qualifies as a near death experience.

I was nine years old at the time, and I believed my dad beat our German Shepard dog to death in the front of me. I thought I was next in line for a beating, too. To me that was considered a near death experience. It sure felt like it. I was frozen in space and could not move. I was in shock. Such a tragic experience as that can be labeled as a near death experience. I was nine years old at the time. We lived on a small farm. The landlord who lived in town had a German Shepard named Prince.

The owner said he was well trained, except he had a bad habit of going after the neighbors chickens. The neighbor complained, and the owner asked my dad if we could keep him since we lived in the country with no close neighbors. But we did have farm animals, chickens, steers and pigs. My dad wanted the dog kept chained up as he did with all the dogs my mother would bring home as puppies. They were to be chained up away from the house as soon they were full grown. My heart ached for them when they had to be chained up because they cried to be let loose.

Sometimes after a while the chained up dogs would be disappear. There were times when I got home from school, the dog would be gone only for me to find out later that my dad and brother had let it loose and used it for moving target practice. It always broke my heart, and I was always afraid to become attached to them because they disappeared after a while by the hands of my father and brother.

It was hard to hang on to love as I was growing up. My mother took my teddy bear away when I was a toddler, never to be seen again, and not even replaced. I had nothing to hang on to. It broke my heart. And now the dogs were disappearing, so I was afraid to become attached. Such emotional trauma, I found can carry over into your adult life too, that non-trust.

As a favor for the landlord my dad took in Prince, the German Shepard. He was a large dog with a pretty coat of various shades of gray. A large German Shepard, he would follow my mother around when she did the laundry and hung it outside on the clothesline. He would be with me and the neighbor kids when we played outside. He did fine. We had him in the house for a bit and then he too was sentenced by my father to be chained up away from the house. Prince was not used to being chained up, of course. So whenever I stepped outside of the house, he like all the other dogs that we had to chain up, cried and begged to be let loose. One day I was home by myself and as my dad was heading out to the fields, I asked him if I could let the dog loose for a while.

"Just let him loose for a little bit," he ordered, "and keep an eye on him."

Prince begged to be let loose, So I unchained him. He ran around in circles for while in front of me, and when he finally settled down, I played ball with him. He was doing fine. But then either I had to go to the bathroom or the phone rang, so I needed to go in the house. A voice in my head said, and I remembered that dogs were not allowed in the house anymore, so I left him on the porch as I hurried to do my business and get back outside. I should have taken him inside with me as it was a big mistake not too.

I hurried but when I got back outside, Prince was no where to be seen. I walked around the yard and toward the out buildings to look for him. I was walking up to the pig pen as my dad was driving the tractor up the field road. We both saw Prince at the same time jumping over the pig pen fence with a little pig in his mouth. My dad put the tractor away in the shed then told me to round up the dog. It took a while as I called Prince again and again, and he finally came to me. I don't know what ever happened to the little pig. I imagine my dad took care of it. Prince had no blood on his muzzle, so I don't know what happened and my dad never said. I only know he had me call Prince, and when he finally came up to the house, my dad was there too.

"Hold the dog by the collar," my dad ordered. So I did. The dog was big and I was a small for nine years old, so I did not even have to bend over to hold Prince by his collar. My dad walked away toward the tool shed.

"What are you going to do?" I asked as he walked away.

"I'm gonna teach him a lesson," he barked over his shoulder at me, as he stomped off toward the tool shed. I continued holding the dog by the collar. I watched as my dad came out of the tool shed carrying a huge hammer, I thought maybe he was going to drive a stake in the ground and tie the dog up to it. I was wrong. Instead my dad walked up to me and took the dog by the collar with his left hand, then he straddled the dog and with his right hand, he began beating the dog over the head with that heavy spike driving hammer.

I stood frozen in shock and fear. I could not move. I thought I would be next in line, because I had let the dog loose and it killed one of dad's little pigs. My dad proceeded to beat the dog over the head at least twelve times, or until he got tired of beating him, and then he let the dog slump to the ground. I remember that the dog looked at me as if to say, "what did I do?" or was that me saying that? I was in shock. I do remember the dog looking at me. I could not move. It felt like I stood there for a long time. Finally, my dad barked an order that woke me up.

"Get in the house," he commanded. I slowly walked up the porch steps and went inside. My mother just sat at the table and said nothing. In silence I walked past her and headed upstairs to my room. I remember lying on the bed still in shock thinking, that I was only nine years old and had at least ten more years to live here with these people.

And then I saw a vision of a spirit. A lovely woman with light curly hair and glasses, but I wasn't to meet her in the physical until many years later. But, lying on that bed, I realized that I was not alone in the world, that I had spirit guides to help protect me. I also felt like I did not belong. I felt other-worldly like I was on a mission here on Earth for something.

The dog beating incident woke something up in me. Yes it felt like a near death experience. And I no longer felt alone. I think my Pleiadian guides were with me from then on as I learned the things they wanted me to, while I was growing up. Seems they sure did not want me to create karma by getting married, that would have me reincarnate back to Earth in the future especially if I had children.

One particular Sunday when I was about eleven, I was standing in the kitchen near the table, where my mother was carving the fat off of a chuck roast that she was going to brown on the top of the stove. As she was carving she was also arguing about something with my dad. They probably were arguing about money, or she wanting him to fix something in the house, or go somewhere with her, like to a wedding. She never knew if he was going to go with her, if not I was usually her sidekick. He was going in and out of the kitchen to the bathroom, finally he just walked out the door to do his chores. My mother was angry.

"I'd like to take this knife," she angrily said, "stick it in him, twist it, and watch the blood run."

"I'm never getting married," I heard myself say out loud, and under my breath I said, "and live like you." I had definitely made up my mind that day at age eleven not to marry and I never did. That incident shook me up. To this day, I never leave a sharp knife laying out on the kitchen counter. After I use it, I immediately wash it and put it back in the drawer. Another reason probably being, is that when I was a kid, and my mom and dad went out at night, while I was sitting up watching TV, I could have the door locked, but when I went to bed I had to unlock the door, so my mom and dad could get back in.

We lived on a small farm near the railroad tracks. And yes, there was a time, when we first moved there, that my mother put her hand on the door knob from inside while a bum or hobo, we called them, coming down the track, had entered our yard and had his hand on the doorknob, too. My mother called my dad from the other room, and he dealt with the bum. Usually Dad made them a sandwich and told them to move on. He was afraid they would camp out in the barn, so he wanted to give them something. No wonder I have occasional flashbacks of Post Traumatic Stress Disorder (PTSD) having to unlock the door before I went to bed.

My childhood has left some PTSD symptoms, for sure. More recently around 2012 I was with my friend visiting her friend who lived on a farm. As we three stood and talked, her husband came walking up to us leading their dog. I saw the man's work pants, his work shoes. I saw the dog. I was out of there. I backed up several yards to get away, my heart racing. I suspect it was a PTSD episode brought on from when I was nine and my dad made me watch him beat, Prince, our German Shepard dog to death.

Another time, was when I was visiting my friend in Tucson, in 2014. She had one of the glue strips that trap rodents. She had it inside her garage. A snake crawled on it and was stuck. I walked out there just in time to see her hack at it with a shovel. Again, I was out of there, I took off running practically out into the street. A PTSD reaction I suppose.

Another time was more recent in the Spring of 2019. I was loading things in my car, and a neighbor walking by told her husband to help me. He had me fold the back seat forward. I did not like having my back to him. I hurried to move the seat and get away, I wanted to face him, where I could see him. He wasn't a dangerous man, just a man, but he had on work shoes and denim work pants which triggered my PTSD. Those are the PTSD events that I recall.

I had a weird experience around 1998 when I and my best friend lived in a log home. I was alone in my bedroom sleeping, when suddenly I was frightened awake, and unable to move, as I felt a warm hand on my waist. It felt as if they were facing me and using their left hand, as I felt like the thumb was closest to my breast. It might have been a friendly Pleiadian but it frightened me. And I think when it realized that it scared me, then it disappeared. kI remember an image of a slender figure dressed in a white hooded gown. I did not get a good look at its face. All I know is that I could not move out of surprise and fear, when I felt the warm hand on my waist. The figure disappeared when it realized that it frightened me. And after a few minutes, finally, I could bring myself to move. I was shaken to the core.

The log cabin was in a wooded area high on the bluffs of the Mississippi River, east of St. Louis, on the west end of Belleville, IL. At the time, other people living along those bluffs were experiencing weird sounds, and we did too. Sounds that sounded like two medal trash cans clanging together. And at that time a police office near Collinsville, IL reported a UFO sighting. Collinsville is along the same bluffs just a few miles north of the log home.

I think things may have had a harsh effect on me because of my PTSD, but even though I did not know it at the time, I probably had my Pleiadians guides watching out over me. Actually, that visitor that night in the log home, may have been a Pleiadian. I felt it was tall slender and wore white or a very light color outfit. I did not see a face as there may have been a large hood pulled forward a bit. It sure felt like an actual visit, as I felt the warm hand on me. It was not a dream, although I had been reading about extraterrestrials. I recall at the time that I listened to the famous after midnight Coast to Coast AM radio show with George Noory as I drove home after working the four to midnight shift at the phone company, I loved learning about those types of things.

It was about then too, that I began to read more and become more aware of the Pleiadians especially around 2005. Years later in 2015 when they told me in that mediumship class with the two instructors that I was from Alcyone of the Pleiades, I really felt connected to them. So I guess these traumatic times during my childhood set me on my path with the metaphysical. Unbeknownst to me at the time, I believe that the Pleiadians were guiding me toward learning all things metaphysical and Astrology. I was drawn to Barbara Marciniak who channeled the Pleiadians. Seems I was on a path to learn more about them as I began studying intuition to learn to become a medium.

I believe those traumatic events kicked my psychic into my higher connection with my Pleiadian guides. I always felt safe and never alone after that. I did not know of course back then that I was a starseed from Alcyone of the Pleiades. But, I felt special, protected, and wiser than most, even way back when I was in grade school. It seemed to me that most of the kids at school were not as intuitive as I was. I saw things differently, I was more in tune with the other side of the veil. I felt spiritual presence, that I was not alone.

When I was very young, I always felt and I realized the eerie truth that the world was very patriarchal, and that white men had white women put into a second class category. White women were considered second class citizens, and were grouped in with all the other minorities. Which made me think that maybe white men did not like their own white women, certainly did not see them as equal.

I also knew that the second class women of the patriarchal system of Aryan males were under a man's thumb, and that was not for me. I would not marry when I grew up; no way was I going to live under some man's thumb. I did not marry, nor did I have any children. And now I realize why I felt that way. Because I have learned I am from Alcyone of the Pleiades which is seventy-five percent female, and only twenty-five percent male, and most importantly, women are in control. And since women are in control, there is no greed, or competition, or hate. Everyone is cooperative and works together for the greater good of all.

I see the patriarchal order rule, the evil that goes on, wars, toxic foods, pills and such. I began to read books by David Icke and others. And have come to believe that some men are evil reptilian humanoid hybrid who are leaders that are in control on Earth. I feel threatened.

It appears to me they are trying to slowly poison humans and kill us off through the GMO foods to weaken our immune systems, make us sick, and send us to the for-profit allopathic medical system. Where mind-controlled brain washed doctors hand out pills that are mere band aids to make us feel better but not necessarily do us any good. Sometimes, I wonder why people would even want to bring children into what I feel is becoming an even a more lopsided, unbalanced society. It is becoming more obvious to me every day that more evil is running the show. It seems to me that the patriarchal rewrote the Bible to suit themselves, and then created all the laws and rules to suit themselves. I think I saw the imbalance even before I learned I was from the Pleiades. My guides and Pleiadians guides have always guided and protected me from harm, and I am most grateful to try to live my life as holistic and organic as possible to maintain my good health.

Chapter Nineteen:

Going Holistic

As I write this in January of 2024, I have hope for a better future for mankind. Because after the c19 jab debacle, I feel and sense that people are waking up to the truth revelation. For the first time in history, the evil reptilian humanoid hybrid elites like the Illuminati, are beginning to be exposed to the public. More and more people have awakened and are beginning to speak out on social media platforms. Many books are being published regarding the obvious corruption in government and corporate and their inhumane ways of putting profits over the health and safety of the people. As I have read in *The 13 Satanic Bloodlines Paving the Road to Hell* by Robin de Ruiter, I think for years since the beginning of the illuminati, that the globalist elites have been planning for a one world government.

A one world government where the cabal rules over our every thought and action. At this time and as I write this, I fear the global health care system which is totally for their profit and everyone else's continuing health decline. Seems it is succeeding in presenting threats of virus for the purpose of stripping away more and more of our freedoms. Since the c19 untested dangerous jab debacle people are beginning to see that the health care system is floundering. More people and more people are switching and going to holistic doctors and being weaned off of dangerous chemical-based medicines. This time the allopathic health care system we have got too daring and pushed meds that were not properly tested. They got too greedy and went too far with a threat of a dangerous virus, when the real threat was in the emergency use mandated untested jabs.

Another obvious clue was the fact that the drug companies could not be sued. That and the fact that Food and Drug Administration (FDA) allowed big chemical to come up with GMO foods in the first place. My Pleiadian guides had me see through the smoke and mirrors. If our government was so worried about our health, why did they allow FDA to pass toxic GMO foods. And why were the jabs free, since when does a for-profit so called health care industry offer anything that is free? And why mandate an untested for emergency use only jab, without liability where they could not be used. Those facts alone should have raised many red flags for people. It only makes me wonder, just what will they try next in order to stripe away more freedoms. I know digital ID for monetary transactions are part of the next plan to control our lives where we will only be able to buy what the digital card allows us to buy.

It's happening already in Canada. These ID digital debt chips or cards have restrictions. Step out of line and your money will be cut off, and no one can give you any of theirs. As all monetary transactions will be strictly monitored. I asked my Pleiadians guides to send help and have the Galactic Federation to come to our aid. So we hope help gets here quickly as it is now the age of Aquarius of feminine rule, and patriarchal rule should be deceasing; anyway we hope. It time for women to clean up men's messes.

People are seeing the fifth dimension Aquarian feminine rule awakening light shine on the truth, and not a moment too soon. I believe more and more people are now going to holistic health care. Holistic health care is natural healing without toxic meds that some are petroleum black tar heroin based, of course petroleum, in the form of polyethylene glycol so its in everything. I heard our allopathic modern day medicine was a mere band aid approach to you feeling good, while the main root of your problem was not tended to. So a nice pain pill so you do not feel the pain or discomfort, although the root of your problems remain unattended to haunt you later on when the condition gets progressively worse.

Seems to me that more and more medical personnel are switching over to holistic herb, vitamin, minerals and nourishing food for building up our immune system in order to ward off illness. There is no money for for-profit allopathic medicine if people are healthy. So they push polyethylene glycol based pills and jabs on the public to drum up business and they do the same with toxic genetically modified organisms (GMO) fake toxic foods being pushed on the public. High fructose corn syrup comes from GMO corn and it is in all your snack products and soft drinks. And Aspartame is a toxin and was FDA passed, so it is in all diet sodas. I don't know why I get the feeling they are trying to bump us off, in some slow unsuspecting, attack of weakening our immune defenses and causing sickness. Talk about an inside job! Nothing like poisoning people to make them sick to drum up more business for allopathic medicine.

Since the c19 bad jabs debacle, I read where the mortuaries report death aimed to appear as death by natural causes are on the rise. The whole idea is to have deaths reported as natural deaths, without anyone being the wiser, that possibly its the food, pills and jabs having causing the harm. Brainwashing also helps as they program us and tell us that we all get sick when we get older or that seems now days it is natural for young children to have heart problems or get cancers.

This never used to be that way, I can't help but feel like it is a war on the people. I suspect all those baby jabs, usually bout twenty-five jabs by the time babies get to age two, and a total of at least seventy-four jabs, by age eighteen. And I read somewhere now that they have added the c19 jab to the children's line up. I recently heard a doctor again saying that vaccines never did work and are not doing anyone any good health-wise. Iin 1957 *The Poisoned Needle, Suppressed Facts about Vaccination* was published by Eleanor McBean.

Like the old saying, when you have a hammer, everything is a nail. Our allopathic medical system seems to have become addictive to using pills and jabs that in the long run do more harm than good as humans are made up of vitamins and minerals not chemicals. But it appears that our US economy at this time in history appears to be fully based on for-profit medicines and humans are collateral damage experiencing deteriorating health. Is all this part of the plan towards evil reptilian humanoid hybrids in control ways to their New World Order of a Totalitarianism world and one religion, that I have read will be Luciferianism? What else are we to think by what we are witnessing at this time.

After over one-hundred-twenty years of allopathic medical deceit and the pushing of money making, "keep-'em coming back for more"pills and jabs. Where is the law to protect the people. I see no laws to protect the people. The FDA seems to have been bought by the very industries they are to oversee. I saw this beginning back in the early 1990's when Aspartame and High Fructose Corn Syrup was passed by Congress and used in sodas, neither is good for your health. Are these mere corrupt methods used just to bring down the human body so you do not feel well and go to the doctor, who of course will give you seven minutes of his time; which, is just time enough to prescribe a pill, not for a cure, but a band aid of a pain pill or anxiety pill band aid. Either of which can be addictive and keeps you coming back for more. So you feel good while what ails your body gets worse inside of you. Its best to learn all that you can. May I suggest watching *"Painkiller"* on Netflix all about Purdue paying off Curtis Wright the FDA man, doctors were encouraged to buy Purdue stock so of course they were going to push their best money maker which was Oxycontin, which just happens to be a schedule two narcotic. In other words a street narcotic made legal. Why have the drug dealers on the street corner making money when big pharmaceutical companies can reap the riches.

As I write this in the beginning of 2024, I have learned through the Pleiadians that the Galactic Federation has many spacecrafts surrounding planet Earth, waiting to be summoned to help us. I asked them to help us as many others are asking for their assistance. I know the government won't as the destructive evil reptilian humanoid hybrids are the ones in control poisoning the air, food, and water and big chemical won't rest until they end everything that is organic, including humans. It is apparent to me that we have evil reptilian humanoid hybrids posing as humans in control allowing a free for all of toxins to be sold. Because corporations use their big bucks to buy off the FDA, and I am sure the EPA too, and whatever other government agency that can best serve them.

When the corporations run the government then we have what is called a fascist government. In my opinion, it is already a dictatorship. I am a Pleiadian on a mission, and the Pleiadians have me look at how government cuts big corporate taxes. Look at how government gives grants to big pharmaceutical companies to develop their jabs and drugs. Those grants are created with our tax dollars. So big corporate gets discovery and development grants and we pay for their products with our diminishing health which just drums up more business for them. The Pleiadians had to observe that the c19 jabs left many with horrendous side effects that doctors turn a blind eye to and say they can't do anything, but give the victim anti-anxiety pills that end up with additional side effects and or maybe an addiction to deal with. So that tells me anxiety pills like Xanax has petroleum in them. Concentrated petroleum is possibly black tar heroin which is addictive.

There was a documentary on Netflix called "*Take your Pills.*" It was all about how patients on Xanax could not get off of it, without having horrible side effects. The same happened with Oxycontin on the Netflix documentary "*Painkiller.*" And I believe nothing much has changed for over a hundred years as petroleum appears to be sweet and addictive, so that is your painkiller band aid when they talk about pills being mere band aids and never getting to the root of the cause of the problem.

Eventually, I read too, that those petroleum based pain pills over time can lead to cancer. So then the patient gets put on more toxins of chemotherapy and radiation treatments. I think plain old common sense tells us that we are not made up of oil or chemicals. Can it get any worse? Yes it can, because according to Jonathan Otto, snake venom is in the jabs. When I read an article on his site and saw the war "venom" I was appalled, I backed up a screen and saw "snake venom" in the c19 jabs. I thought that cannot be an accident. Earlier when I read about all the horrendous side effects some people got from the c19 jabs, I gave them a benefit of a doubt that maybe lab accidents happened. But who brings a vile of snake venom into a lab by mistake.

I began learning about spike protein I guess from the snake venom causing crazy side effects. It seems that when the jab hit the vein that lethal thick unnatural blood clot forms in vein, I saw videos of such on Jonathan Otto from autopsies. Alongside the blood clots were long strands of Flex Seal like white material. The doctors on the video were puzzled, they had never before seen anything like it. And then I heard about people getting masses and tumors in their head. And I imagined that when the jab needle missed the vein the serum went from the arm to the head causing strange masses to form. Just my thinking of why there were different weird conditions showing up after getting the jabs.

So now adding snake venom to the water supplies, guess fluoride is working fast enough. So then later on, I learned via Dr. Bryan Ardis that besides having fluoride added to our city's drinking water systems now snake venom will be added. He said to counter the effect of the snake venom that nicotine should be used. Like nicotine patches or gums, Melatonin should be taken. Foods that contain nicotine are pineapples, raisins, plums, potatoes, cabbage, black pepper and all other peppers.

My wonderful Pleiadians guides gave me an idea and had me like the taste of adding organic lemon juice, cayenne pepper, and organic maple syrup to my water bottle everyday for at least six years now. See how they have helped protect me. And they gave me the idea to only eat organic foods. I feel very special and blessed to have them have my back. I think too, besides the obvious vortex effect is that they wanted me away from the going along with the propaganda of the crowd mentality regarding the c19 debacle. So I know I am in the Southwest on a mission to do my *DianneTheMedium* podcast on PodBean and to write this book to help people be awakened and enlightened as to make an easier transition into the Aquarian feminine rule of the fifth dimension where love will over rule the evil. Enough negativity, back to my wonderful Pleiadian guidance.

My Pleiadians guides are the best, recently I was really missing my friend who moved back east. It seemed we had drifted apart a bit, after we had enjoyed many walks, hikes, shopping and biking adventures before she moved away. I was a medium for her pasted cousin to come forward and relate messages to her. He is still with me, I know he encouraged me to text her and so I finally did. I feel so much better and feel that she and I still have a soul to soul connection via her cousin's connecting us. We had a lengthy texting conversation. After we both called it a night, as it was getting late, I happened to walk into the other room and saw 11:11 on the clock, to me that was a thumbs up and a loving smile from my Pleiadian guides and that made me smile even more. Seems the more I see the signs from my guides, the closer I am with them and their many magical signs and gifts.

May I take the liberty to suggest to everyone who reads this to get to know your guides. Find a nice quiet place, maybe in a park where you can be alone to meditate. Just for your own feelings of comfort and safety, say, "only the good guides." Then ask your guides to come forward and ask them, "What do I call you? I wish to know you." To feel even more confident if you are a bit skeptic about communicating with spirits from the other side then say "only the good spirits come forward." And spirits need to honor your wishes. Develop a loving relationship and be grateful for them.

I thank my wonderful guides Rosie, Emma, Steve and the Pleiadians throughout the day. The more you connect with them, the more you will see the magic of their love for you. As I reflect on the recent event with Steve and contacting his cousin, I now realize that my Pleiadian guides had me stay and not go to my usual Monday event. Steve had me really missing her and I did ask him to reconnect her and I, and then I kind of forgot about it. I think Steve picked the best time for her and I to communicate, and that was he made me feel like staying home. A few minutes after I made up my mind to stay home, I got the sudden urge that it was a good time to text her. Later I realized that Steve probably thought it was a good time for me to contact her, and that she was in a good place, and I believe that is why it went so well. I thanked Steve and my guides. And then I got a response back from them as they had me walk into the next room and I see 11:11 on the clock. That is a good sign "it's a go" magical sign. I am so fortunate to have my guides and the Pleiadians with me in these scary times.

Yes these are scary times. But at the same time, the Galactic Federation along with their Pleiadian members have encircled their spacecraft around Earth and are just helping. I welcome them to come in and straighten out their mess that they created twelve thousand five hundred years ago when they placed the computerized moon above Earth to hold Earth in the third dimension, which was fine, until the reptiles decided to emerge from the depth of Earth to mingle with the humans on the surface. They quickly learned how to hack the Moon's computer and tweet it, to make life on Earth more harsh for the humans as they discovered they could steal DNA from the white human male and create a Reptilian Humanoid Hybrid and create those thirteen Satanic, without a soul or conscious, bloodlines. And without a conscious or soul they scratched and clawed their way into high positions of government and corporations.

So it explains the evil actions we see happening today. And it seems to me that they are becoming more daring and blatant. Seems to me that they are trying to poison humans into extinction. The health system now in control had bought up media and bad mouthed holistic teaching medical school of Cornell University about a hundred and fifty years ago calling it quackery. And the world still runs on oil, so it is in everything from vehicles to pills, jabs, plastics, vinyl and in the way of polyethylene glycol, an antifreeze. The Pleiadians have led me to learn that the flu and c19 jabs consisted of formaldehyde, for preservation, polyethylene glycol is used so nano particles do not stick together and its used to spark the immune system. Well, I guess so it would, since it is toxic! Also there is mercury and probably aluminum. The EPA has allowed, for years now, fluoride, the waste product of manufacturing aluminum to be dumped into most cities across the country water supplies. Why I wonder, do rats reside there? Read the back of a box of d-CON brand of rat poison, fluoride is listed, right? It is the brand of a popular rat poison used all over the world.

I remember when I was right out of high school in the late 1960's and had just finished beauty culture school, got my license, and was working in my mother's beauty salon in our small southern Illinois town. I remember the day, my Pleiadians, had me remember it for today, and this book I'm sure. I remember the day I was doing Rita B's hair. Her husband was a scientist for Alcoa Aluminum in East St. Louis, IL. I remember her telling me that they dumped fluoride, the waste product of manufacturing aluminum, right into surrounding small town drinking water supplies. See, my Pleiadian guides had me remember that. And then they even put it in toothpaste and still do.

Then they had the government and the AMA dentist

had the unethical audacity to tell us that fluoride prevented cavities. Which was an absolute falsehood. Now isn't that a crime? When the opposite is true, it wrecks your bones and causes cavities. Just another way to drum up business for the medical system. Isn't poisoning people a crime against humanity? Where is the law? Read *Fluoride the Aging Factor* by Dr. John Yiamouylannis first published 1983.

In the book *Humans Get Off Your Knees*, David Icke speaks of the controlling computerized Moon matrix and how its frequencies control reptilian humanoid hybrid males throughout the world to turn against women. Patriarchal government and societies are global. What does that tell you, they all got the same message somehow many centuries back, even thousands of years ago. Remember, I had written earlier that the reptile females had had enough from the renegade males and locked out all the reptilian males from Lyra.

Well, turns out reptiles do not forget or forgive and pass their hatred on to human women by sending out from the Moon mind manipulating and controlling frequencies that programs reptilian humanoid hybrid males. And those programs are creating various degrees of ADHD, nervous and therefore recklessness. As nervous, angry, in a hurry, males become big pickup truck owners, who become tailgaters and impatient males honking at motorist to make them move up into the intersection so he can make sure he makes the left turn light. From my observation, it seems they all have narrow vision and only see and hear what they want to in order to serve themselves. Their only concern is getting their way right now and they see women as prey, to be controlled, manipulated and dominated.

For example, by creating birth control devices and not testing them properly or in the case of a group of women in their test group. The altered their surveys to push through the FDA process. So these foreign material made devices were not properly tested or proven to be safe before they inserted them into women's bodies. The women soon developed fevers as their bodies tried to reject the foreign object which could not be removed totally as the device would break apart into tiny pieces. Which of course later caused horrendous autoimmune diseases. This medal long thin screw like device was called Ensure and after thousands of injured women stormed on Washington, the product was left on the market to be prescribed by doctor's discretion for two more years, until 2018. Many women developed auto immune disease as devices like the Ensure birth control metal device gets so embedded in human tissue, it cannot be removed, or breaks in pieces when attempted. Instead of men getting vasectomies that can easily be reversed if necessary. Even in modern times seems the medical system makes it difficult for the mother to deliver her baby. making woman lie down to make it more convenient for the attending physicians. When common sense seems that squatting and using gravity and water births would make so much more sense. And it seems to me that the patriarchal ran government has a great desire to control women's health and reproductive rights. Plain to me, generally speaking that It is truly a patriarchal rule society and males rule over women's bodies forbidding abortion. Women have to beg the court room of men, even if medical conditions threaten the mother's life along with the babies, to grant her permission to get an abortion. Why in this the twenty-first century, must a woman go to court and beg for an abortion if in a case where there is a sick fetus that is endangering her very own health too. She has to wait for the men to decide. Where mostly male judges being selected to the Supreme Court where the likes of conservative judges who delayed decisions of granting an abortion or not, obviously playing god and trying to force the woman to carry the fetus to term.

My Pleiadian family has brought these atrocities done on to women to my attention. I have my DianneTheMedium.com web site and my *DianneTheMedium* podcast on PodBean, to help enlighten and awaken humans into the Aquarian feminine rule of the fifth dimension we are presently in. So women need to rise up to equal status and then beyond, just don't take it anymore. Remember back before 1969 women were tested to see if they could handle being in space. They all fared better than the men even when it came to math. Remember the movie *Hidden Figures*. However women did not get their chance to go into space, since we live in a patriarchal society.

The Galactic Federation spacecrafts have encircled Earth and are waiting for we humans to summons them to help dominate over and make the evil Reptilian

Humanoid Hybrids docile and to stop their becoming more and more aggressive with their blatantly obvious attacks on humans. Not just in this country but globally now with this c19 debacle of treatments and toxic jabs either injuring, maiming for life, or killing people in unknown numbers. The total death count by these so-called emergency use approved, can't be sued, poorly or untested jabs injury counts will never be learned.

The Pleiadian wish is that soon hopefully all humans see that these without conscious or soul, cruel and evil, reptilian humanoid hybrids in powerful positions do exist. Surely anyone can see these men in powerful positions create wars and where banks gain to profit by funding both sides. I can't help but think that they don't care how many innocent people are maimed and killed. They have no regards for women and children, as they brutally rape, torture and butcher them. So very obvious to me, they who are in charge, are certainly not human with a conscious or soul.

The problem with the world is that it is ran by patriarchal self-serving greedy evil white reptilian humanoid hybrid satanic worshiping mostly white men. And of course, they are racist and sexist, even group their own white women in the minorities category, as second citizens. Just look at the Bible that apparently to me has been rewritten by the white reptilian humanoid hybrid males to dominate over all women even their own white women. White women are considered second class citizens, they have grouped in with all the other races, making it obvious to me that white male reptilian human hybrids never have forgotten how reptilian females locked out the males form Lyra. So it is quite obvious to me that yes indeed some males in high position and otherwise are controlled by the computer on the Moon sending out certain frequencies for the purpose of mind control. Just like HAARP they say controls all the weather.

Just look at the world in general especially in the United States. No one speaks of it, but everyone thinks that 9/11 was an inside job to take down the towers. The planes were just for the well positioned cameras that caught all the actions, before the planted high-tech Tesla like explosives took down the two towers, even the short number seven building that was not hit by a plane. Remember all the dust instead of debris. Read *Where Did the Towers Go?* by Judy Wood. Find and watch GAIA Conscious Media Network interview with engineer Judy Wood. Indeed, scary times of deceasing freedoms and forced upon tightening restrictions.

The Pleiadians have brought my attention to the powers that be that seem to be trying to gear us towards global health care and a New World Order Poppy Bush always wanted. It had been reported that his eyes that could turn to yellow make slits, Yes Poppy Bush. Junior did not call him Poppy Bush for nothing as Poppy had troops guarding Afghanistan poppy fields to make cocaine for street use. Read or better yet listen to Cathy O'Brien read the audible book *Trance-formation of America* how during the mid-1980s when she was a mere MK Ultra sex slave for Gerald Ford and his buddies in the White House as they raped and tortured her while snorting cocaine on the presidential desk. Poppy Bush was there, Reagan too, he liked to call her, Kitten. They knew to say the Walt Disney words "follow the yellow brick road" to put her mind controlled into a sexual trance while they raped her, sometimes so brutally sending her to medical care. And then they would give her shock treatments in attempt to make her forget, read the book. Better yet listen to it, as she reads it.

Watch her Regina Meredith Conscious Media Network interview Season Three episode forty, her co-author and rescuer Mark Phillips interview is episode thirty-eight. So doesn't Moon matrix mind programming of these thugs in power make sense that they are indeed reptilian humanoid hybrids and they are attempting to mind control us, with television shows, music and brain-washing commercials. It is getting even more scary. My Pleiadian family brings these things to my attention so I can podcast on *DianneTheMedium* at Podbean.

I have noticed lately four different movies on Netflix about the end of the world. What is that all about? Why about the end of the world? Are they trying to tell us something? The first one I watched was Meryl Streep in *"Don't Look Up."* There is a meteor approaching Earth and two scientists try to warn Meryl Streep playing the cigarette smoking president. It might to be dark comedy. At the end it shows family sitting around a dinner table chit chatting has the house begin to shat and shatter from the energy of the approaching meteor.

146

Another is "*Leaving the World Behind*" with Julia Roberts and of all people, why is it co-produced by the Obama's. Yes. Watch it. The music is frightening and bazaar as is the movie, and hopefully not mind controlling, but one never knows. I watched the one movie where the guy is driving back to Seattle to find his wife only when he gets there it is all destroyed. I believe that is called "This Is How it Ends." And then there is "*Carol and the End of the World*" an animated movie series about just that, the end. Why? Are they trying to make us comfortable with the thought of the possibly of a impending doomsday disaster.

I just heard a guru on a reel on Facebook say that the fifth dimension is on the other side of the veil. I know Delores Cannon had said that we will be lighter eating less, and that that fifth dimension is light. When I heard her saying that, I wondered does she mean we will all be dead? Is that what the four end of the world movies are about, a hint as to what is to come?

We know the reptiles feed on human fear. Which brings me to religion or shall I say cult. I have read that all religions are a cover up, a facade, for satanic rituals; baby eating rituals. I got another one for you to watch that is on Netflix, watch "*Keep Sweet Pray and Obey*" about Warren Jeffs, in Part two or three, he gets very angry and his eyes turn to yellow snake eyes. Here is proof that reptiles rewrote the Bible to suit themselves by having a serpent, makes sense right, to tempt Eve, of course the women, blame it on the woman, Eve. So she temps Adam with the apple that gets them driven out of paradise and from then on women according to the Bible have to suffer painful childbirth. So of course the words goes down patriarchal lines to the allopathic medical schools and how to make women lay down during childbirth and they get epidurals in their spine, which brings them back to the for-profit medical system in a few years with back trouble. So they get operated on and possibly get a drop foot out of it. But women are wising up and rising up.

As two women lab techs, merely took the PCR test out of the box and put it in the machine to see the results, without even being used the tests came back positive. Are you finally catching on? We get vitamin D from the sun and vitamin D is important to work with cholesterol that our brains need. Recently I read on page 114 in *Pleiadian Perspective* by Amorah Quin Yin, that the sun is a gateway to communication to Alcyone of the Pleiades and to the Galactic Center. I know that my guides and my Pleiadian family led me to that book just so I would open it up on page 114 and see the message they wanted me to see.

Now I know why I always want to get out in the sun every day possible. My Pleiadians tell me that there are good spirits of light and there are evil spirits of darkness. There are evil reptile brains of the Illuminati using their puppet slaves reptilian humanoid hybrids they created and planted everywhere around the world to reack havoc of humans. The evil ones keep humans unaware that they are mere victims and subjects of the evil empire of satanic rituals, the younger and more frightened the blood and flesh, the better they like it.

There are portals down into the Earth where the reptiles hide; but, they getting ever more eager to expose themselves to humans and roam the surface of Earth in their true reptilian form as they had created reptilian humanoid hybrid that have the capability to shape shift to appear human; but, they never could replicate the human emotions has they have no soul. When humans die, only their bodies die, their souls live on. But when reptiles die, that's it.

I think and I believe the Pleiadians tell me that the reptiles of the illuminati tired to replicate human soul consciousness but cannot, and that is why they hate that they cannot kill humans. The reptiles even try to duplicate humans by building androids and robots. The evil ones wish to control every move the humans make, their health, their food, and they wish to make everyone use a digital card that they have the control over your health, your purchases. And they can cut you off at anytime, if you try to step out of line. Sounds a little like communist China. But we have help on the horizon.

Chapter Twenty:

Galactic Federation to the Rescue.

The Galactic Federation has encircled Earth at the end of 2023 and are eager to be summons. The Pleiadians are members of the Galactic Federation and have led me to so I see certain articles and people in news reels on Facebook where the Galactic Federation revealing that the Galactic Federation have indeed positioned spacecraft encircling the globe eager to come to our rescue. Pleiadians, I say, ask the Galactic Federation to not wait to be summons I ask just get here. Because all in powerful positions are reptilians. There is no one to summons them, except we starseeds that they have sent here to observe, monitor and report back. And the Galactic Federation needs to be our heroes our knights in shining armor and either shut down the Moon's computer that is controlling behavior on Earth or neutralize the reptilian brain. I believe that the Pleiadians wanted me to know this, so I was led to learn and I came to believe that the Moon's frequencies controls the reptilian humanoid hybrid males in powerful position behavior. I am a starseed form the 'Alcyone of the Pleiades here with the rest of the starseeds to help awaken and enlighten all humans on planet Earth.

Chapter Twenty-One:

Pleiadians Hints and Messages

I thank my Pleiadians guides and Rosie, Emma, and Steve all day long when I think of ways they have helped me throughout the day. I love the way they direct me to certain things they want me to see, learn and read. Like when straightening up or moving my stacks of books around, I am drawn to a certain book: *Pleiadian Perspectives on Human Evolution*, by Amorah Quan Yin for a reason. So, I look through my page number locations that I had written in the beginning of the book. I am drawn to page 114 where I read that the sun is a gateway to communications to Alcyone of the Pleiades and is a gateway to communications to the Galactic Center. And that Light Beings are from the Galactic Center and from Alcyone, the central Sun of the Pleiades. Alcyone had been chosen long ago as the main control and monitoring station for lifeforms in our solar ring, so it was natural to continue in that role.

There is a reason I am gay. On Page 67 I learned as I read the Pleiadian teachers say a person needs sexual healing, that if they were molested and the person has become too damaged to heal sexually with the opposite gender because trust and safety have been destroyed. So a person later in the same life time or in the next life time chooses a same-sex partner and two wonderful things can happen. First, in the atmosphere of having the same qualities of trust and respect after a while that can be restored. Secondly, as the person receives and gives love to the same gender he or she begins to appreciate peoples' unique qualities that are gender specific. So they learn they have the same qualities. From there then they learn self-respect, self-love and self-trust are developed, or reborn, and the person starts to let go of guilt, shame, anger, low self-worth, and victim/victimizer scenarios.

So the individual then realizes that they are lovable and tender and as wonderful as their partner is, and so learn to deserve respect too. And won't ever settle for less than that ever again. They have learned the value of what they had to offer because they have been receiving the same from their gay partner. So learning this, I was especially inspired with hope that I do get updates from the Pleiadians each day when I get out into the sunshine.

As I said earlier, on page 114 it says that the Sun is a gateway communications to Alcyone of the Pleiades and is also a gateway to the Galactic Center which is located at 26 degrees in the sign of Sagittarius. So I try to get out in the sun everyday. My Pleiadian guides help me in my timing. Like go early because it will be cloudy in the afternoon even thus the weather app indicates it will be sunny all day. So I find it's right on, that when I get back home right before it clouds up. My guides and Pleiadian family direct me dearly all day long. Like the best time to hike, before the clouds roll in.

Like certain things they wish to see on television as I write this in January 2024. And I have found more gloom and doom movies about the end of times. And it makes me wonder or they trying to frighten us, because fear wrecks your immune system and make you more vulnerable to the c19 jab side effects. Or is there something they are trying to prepare us for through Netflix movies: The Pleiadian have drawn my attention to four "end of the World" movies presently being shown on Netflix. The first, "*Carol and the End of the World.*" Where doom comes in a large planetary planet heading for Earth. The second, is "*How It All Ends,*" about a man trying to get back to his wife in Seattle only to find when he finally arrives that all of Seattle is destroyed, by what I am not sure, I guess a meteor. The third is "*Don't Look Up*" where two scientist discover that a large Meteor is heading to earth and they have about six months before total annihilation is enviable and no one believes the two scientist. The fourth movie out on Netflix as I write this is "*Leaving the World Behind*" with Julia Roberts and produced by all people the Obama's. Yes, Barack and Michele.

There are many movies I have watched on Netflix. Seem to me that Netflix is in the helping mankind mode showing the real truths behind American Medical Associations botch jobs and ill-tested devices, if third party tested at all. I cannot help but feel that war has been bestowed on the American people by their very own government. A fascist government owned by the very big corporations.

I feel that I am here at this time to write books and to do my DianneTheMedium.com mediumship readings. So people see our connection with the spirit side across the veil. Also I believe that my Pleiadian guides have directed me to PodBean so I would create my podcast: *DianneTheMedium* at PodBean I also share them on X (Twitter) and on Facebook feeds, Along with my singing and playing my ukulele as I promote the eight books that I have written so far.

Verda being my latest that I publish in January of 2023. It is my take on this whole c19 debacle, I feel with a healthy immune system everyone would have been just fine. It was the jab side effects that appeared to be the real attack on the people , sorry to say. When I heard the jabs were free from a for-profit medical system. A system that has been serving up to the public non-nutritional genetically engineered organisms as food. A system that has allowed untested devices implanted in woman. A system that allows big drug and chemical companies to pay to get things passed by the government so they can push a schedule two narcotic painkiller. I figured they were, and I told my friend as much.

"They're up to something," I warned, paying attention to message from the Pleiadians that I had received. I was trying to persuade her and others, but my words pretty much fell on deaf ears.

Chapter Twenty-Two:

Helping Others

My Pleiadian family has helped guide me on my path to help awaken and enlighten humankind in order to raise above the horrid of these evil reptilian humanoid hybrid ruling patriarchal times by raising our vibrations. Raise your consciousness by getting out in to nature and medicating, appreciating life and your guides. Get to know your guides. Meditate and ask them to come forward and send signs.

Sometimes the Pleiadians and my my guides like to play tricks on me. I always make sure I keep my storage shed locked because I keep my expensive road bike in there. I know it had to be one of them, the day I unlocked the shed door and found a board from the very top shelf across the handlebars and seat of my bike. I am not surprised anymore of the things they do, but I like to tease them right back.

"Pleiadians and guides Rosie, Emma, or Steve who ever did this," I said, "taking a board down from the top shelf may have been fairly easy, I suspect. How about the next time I unlock the shed, I find that the board is off my bike and back on the top shelf."

Of course, each time I checked, the board was not back on the top shelf, and still laying across the handlebars and seat of my bike. I can't reach that top shelf to put the board back, so each time I put my bike back in the shed after I ride it, I place the board back across my handlebars and seat just in case they decide they want to try to put the board back up on the top shelf.

"Let's see you put the board back up on that top shelf." I say as I tease them. So far they have not done that. But I get a kick knowing it was them. I telepathically speak to them all the time. More recently, they pulled another trick on me.

I was lying in bed, and thought to take a vitamin I forgot to take earlier. So I reached down in a bag by my bed. I dug out the bottle of pills. I was laying on my right side close to the edge of the right side of the bed. I held the bottle with my right hand and with my left hand unscrewed the plastic cap. I laid the cap down on the sheet next to me, so I could get a pill out. I heard the cap hit the carpet on the floor by my bed. Or so I thought I did. With my left hand I felt all over the carpet and surrounding floor. I could not find the cap. I gave up and set the opened bottle in a safe place on the nightstand so I wouldn't knock it over. I was puzzled as later when I got up to go to the bathroom, I never stepped on it. The heck with finding the cap I went to sleep.

The next morning after I took my shower, I was

sitting on the side of my bed. Never did see the bottle cap. Three feet away I had my Vibram high-top toe shoes near the closet door. I picked the right one up, to put it on. I found that plastic cap inside my shoe. Go figure. Then I recalled the sound I heard the night before when I thought that cap fell on the carpet right by my bed, or so I thought. It did sound close by. But, when I think of it now, that sound I heard did sound like something hitting nylon material, like my shoe is made out of. Three feet away that shoe was. The cap should have just slid off my sheet that it was lying on next to me. It had to be the Pleiadians, again. Pretty amazing isn't it. No wonder I speak to them all the time. Evidently they are always near me. Then there was the flying fork incident.

I was in St. Louis at my condo. I had people over. It was time to eat. It was taco night. I had been thinking of mind over matter stunts. Like people just using their thoughts to bend spoons and such. So, I said to the Pleiadians, "How about having my fork fly up, or rise up in the air above my plate?" It was a plastic fork, so I thought maybe using my mind, I could do it, or have the Pleiadians help me. I wanted it to happen in front of my guest who I thought were right behind me. But they were still in the kitchen, and no one had returned back to the room yet. So I took my seat. On the way to sitting down with my place in my hand, some how, my hand nipped the plastic fork or so I thought it did. Anyway, the fork when flying in a bigger than necessary arch and landed six feet away by the fireplace. I had to smile.

My Pleiadians did help with the stunt. They make me smile.

I got another magical moment story. I was leaving a cafe parking lot, and backed against a light pole. My heart sank at the sound. I didn't even get out to look at it until I drove the three miles home. When I got home and parked under the street light. My heart sank even more. My driver side back quarter panel, the quarter panel piece from the top of the tail light to the top of the back wheel well, was separated. I went inside. I asked my Pleiadians, "Can't we just pretend like it didn't happen? My car is such a good car, it doesn't deserve this." Rain was due to begin and so I ran down to my car to get the jacket I had left in the car. While I was down there. Something gave me the idea. To just take both of my hands and press that panel back into place. Guess what, it snaps right back into place. Thank you my Pleiadian guides. The next day I used a little touch up paint where there was a scuff on the edge below the tail light. I thanked my guides profusely. And now I am so much more careful. These were action replies. I have already gotten telepathic verbal messages.

It was after Steve spelled out his name in puffs of white clouds against a blue sky when I heard Steve say, "And not Steven." And there was another time when I requested his assistance.

"You are going to have to help me get her over here," I said, "she just got back into town, I don't feel as if I can bother her."

Then telepathically I heard Steve say, "Watch this,"

and I heard it. I was amazed at his power, because within thirty minutes she was texting me.

"What are you doing," she asked, "can I come over?"

So you too can do magical things, try getting in touch with your psychic and spiritual side by taking solo walks out in nature, maybe walk in parks away from the energy and frequencies of people and noise. Sit and meditate and learn to get to know your guides. Everyone can be psychic, a medium, and to channel. I get messages clairvoyantly I see and hear in my mind's eye. Or they direct me to my desire. Suddenly I will feel like that a walk, or taking out my trash or getting the mail right now. And that is so I can run into the potential sitter that my guides want me to get to know.

And more recently it was Steve, the sitter's cousin, who passed when she was twelve and he at age fifteen died in a tragic auto accident back in 1969. Time is not the same on the other side of the veil. A part of Steve's soul might even have gone on to another reincarnation, but a part of his soul remains behind to reconnect and guide his loved ones, like his cousin who lived across the way from me. Steve is my guide now too. I know he watches over his cousin.

At the beginning I was the medium and now since the sitter has moved back east, I tell Steve, you are the medium now between her and me, and trust me, he is. He recently set up a meeting between us. I had asked him to a week or so prior. I told him that I really missed her, I missed her energy. I try to connect with her all the time using telepathically. I do feel that when you think of another loving souls that you once were connected with that they feel that. I know if a living person thinks of a past loved one that is across the veil that that passed loved one then comes forward, and that is connecting across the veil, so I am sure that two loving soul-to-soul connections can certainly mind-to-mind connect telepathically as they feel the other is thinking about them.

When I hike to my rock across the Bell, most times I see her face as it flashes in front of me, if for only a second she comes through plain and clear. Of course mind you, I am sitting on a vortex when I see her, as she may be in her area where she is. I believe she was one of the reasons that Rosie said, "You are the medium, I will bring them forward," in that galley back in 2017. Rosie introduced herself to me not long after the Pleiadians had introduced themselves to me in front of those two witnesses in that classroom that evening around 2015 and evidently they had psychic mediumship plans for me that consisted of not only mediumship readings but mediumship missions, where they found housing for me across from the passed spirits target sitter and in a popular vortex area.

Vortex locations can be felt in several ways. One day I hiked Boynton Canyon and I was climbing to the highest point where people sit. A few feet up ahead of me, in front of me, a young woman asked me, "Where is the vortex?" I told her it is mostly an energy that can not be seen. But expect vortex to be where the small pine type juniper trees are the most twisted.

"I see waves in front of me," she suddenly said.

"I see them too," and I did, I told her that we just witnessed a vortex energy wave and that the Pleiadians are here. We both were amazed and felt blessed that we got to experience such a magical energetic phenomenon. I feel the same magical energy when I am back in St. Louis and ride my bike to Forest Park and feel the vortex that runs through there. I certainly hope to one day again experience another magical moment with a bird, like I wrote previously about. I believe that is the magic of the vortex which is reflecting our higher vibrational spiritual experience as we begin to interface with extraterrestrials and with the spirit world, as we experience life on planet Earth now that we are in the Aquarian feminine rule fifth dimension. I read somewhere that reptilian humanoid hybrid males who are Illuminati slaves of the reptiles living underground. They will dissipate as they cannot survive now that we are in the fifth dimension of peace and love. The evil will be leaving the planet and are going away, and Earth will soon return once again to total organic. Dirty old fashioned petroleum based combustion engines will be replaced with quiet, clean electric or hydrogen fueled powered vehicles. The future is now, so get to know your guides.

May I suggest that you get to know your guides by journaling, meditating, getting out in nature, and out in the sunshine. Even if the skies are slightly overcast. Hopefully, there is a nice breeze to push the toxic chemtrails they are spraying on us out of the way and out of the area. I ask the Galactic Federation to please aid us in our time of desperation. As I had falsely believed that the nasty chemtrails were only be sprayed over the United States, but now I have come to learn recently that spraying chemtrails have gone into high gear and now are sprayed globally. Those heavy thick long lines of clouds are not ordinary airplane condensation, created because as hot engine air meeting the cold air of the stratosphere creates line of condensation; but those naturally occurring condensation clouds are short lived and dissipate quickly. This is the land of the vortex energy that I believe they are trying to block.

Another place I feel the vortex is around Raleigh, NC. I have been there for psychic fairs and to attend Barbara Marciniak's sessions where she channels the Pleiadians at the Dancing Moon bookstore in Raleigh. I believe anyone can be psychic and can be a medium, or a channel. I receive channel messages more and more now, and I have learned to listen for them. The Pleiadians and my guides: Rosie, Emma, and Steve advise me, and they have me on wonderful missions. They have protected me all my life by giving me good common sense, a loving heart and soul, and we starseeds have empathy.

I just saw 2:22 on the clock as I write this, I feel that tells me I am on the right path to share my knowledge and experience to encourage others to meditate to raise your vibrations into the fifth dimension of Aquarian feminine rule. I feel they speak through me as they have given me an excellent memory and superior recall capabilities. So I wish to do their bidding, and we only work with the good spirits. If you, the medium, decide to meditate and enhance your psychic capabilities and feel more confident and safe many times over just say, "Only the good spirits. I will only work with the good spirits." I always speak with my guides and the Pleiadians and thank them for my perfect health and safe travels as I journey across the country.

Of course, I realize I have to do the work, like regularly having good car maintenance done. For example, when the dealer mechanic tells me I will need tires soon, I say, put them on today. I always take my 2016 Prius to the Toyota dealer, because the dealer's mechanics know your car and they know about recalls that may occur.

Just looked up and saw 2:34 on the clock, another message telling me I am on the right track, so I thank them. I have always felt that the Pleiadians have guided me when it came to not choosing to participate in medical systems' brainwashing revolving-door, taking advantage of human health for their monetary gain, only. I have refused flu shots, and certainly, I did not buy into the hype about the c19 toxic jabs, certainly not after I read an article on Jonathan Otto, where Dr Bryan Ardis says that snake venom is in the jabs. I thank my Pleiadian guides profusely for making me not want to get those jabs; making me feel adamant about it, like I would have only gone kicking and screaming. So, beware and hope you don't need a blood transfusion, as people who got the jab these last three years give blood and spread toxins to unsuspecting victims attending health care facilities. Beware!

And didn't Procter and Gamble use a satanic emblem on their product label? Was that a hint? Yes, I believe the evil reptiles have risen up from the depths of the planet to take over and they are succeeding in their efforts to depopulate through illness. Why do you think we have toxins in the air, water, food, and your brain is perhaps controlled by frequencies coming from the moon's computer that the reptiles hacked to make it worse here on Earth for the humans. My Pleiadians have enlightened me via my psychic messages and intuition.

These waves of intuition and just knowing intuitional messages come to me from the Pleiadians or my guides Rosie, Emma, and Steve. I have the most wonderful guides. They lead me to the books they want me to read, and they lead me to the direct page they want me to read. I do feel it is an honor and a privilege to represent Alcyone of the Pleiadians. On Alycone there is seventy-five percent women; therefore, it is run very well. Women are not competitive but rather cooperate and work together for the greater good.

Lynne McTaggaret said that Darwin's theories were misconstrued. Humans are more likely not to be competitive but rather to be cooperative for the greater good. But, the patriarchal have trained reptilian humanoid hybrid males to be competitive, so they are more destructive. In order to save the planet, from the evil reptiles in control, things need to and will change.

So, I suggest that all the Galactic Federation has to do is get rid of the patriarchal rule not only in America, but of the world. Which proves that mankind, made up of reptilian humanoid hybrid males, have Earth being controlled by frequencies coming from the Moon. I realize this is very difficult to even fathom. Planet Earth needs help from the good guys, and I trust that the Galactic Federation will see to it, as will my Pleiadian guides.

I thank my guides, for getting me out of Dodge, as the saying goes, when the c19 scam debacle first began and that was to protect me from negative peer pressure and falsified hearsay. You know "misinformation," is always the opposite of what they say or who they blame. I think I would beware. Haven't you noticed the increase in medical procedures as more people are falling prey to surgeries, it seems to be at an ever increasing rate. I believe trust in our medical system is declining rapidly, especially since the mandated toxic jab attack debacle that caused so many horrendous side effects, permanent damage, even deaths.

I have a theory, I think my Pleiadian guides help me see. Those who had toxic polyethylene glycol, formaldehyde, aluminum, Mercury, and yes snake venom jabs hit a blood vessel, got thick blood clots. But, when autopsies were performed doctors, found alongside the thick blood clots, some Flex Seal type white long clots. And I think people, where the jab did not hit a vessel that caused a stroke, clot and death, who got the jab into muscle, then maybe that is why they got a mass or tumor in their head. Just guessing from information I have read and heard about. My guides are having me think this, too. And I wonder, the snake venom is of course foreign to the human body so did it cause the white stuff and tumors. Of course, formaldehyde and polyethylene glycol is in the jabs too, according to Dr. Bryan Ardis.

With all the brain washing television shows and commercials, I guess I am not surprised that people fall in line and obey. While reading, *Human Beings Get Off Your Knees* by David Icke, I learned that mass mind control has been done on the population as they have been conditioned by the moon matrix, the news, and conditioned by our modern medicine system to just accept these things. It's best to eat organically to keep your immune system built up. And get out in the sunshine. Let's not allow disease and ill health to become so common place the public to accepts cancer as to be a common phenomenon in modern times. But be careful, think positive, exercise and eat organic. Be careful, as your thoughts are very powerful and your body's cells hear your every thought. If you have come to accept that you will probably die of cancer, you will die that way. That is called a self-fulfilling prophecy. J.Z Knight says your thoughts are very powerful as your cells in your body hear your every thought.

Why have we come to put all our trust in the allopathic? We have come to except giving twenty-five vaccines to a baby by the time they are two years old. That's even before their tiny immune systems have developed. And then they get nearly a total of seventy-four jabs these days by the time they are a teenager. And I have read recently where the c19 jab has been added to that vaccine line up.

No wonder young people come down with all sorts of neurological conditions while growing up, or do not feel comfortable in their own skin and wish to change their sex, or be called a gender neutral name. Some people shame those who are gender confused. And when those conditions come up, they never stop to think it might be a side effect from all the jabs the medical system pricked them with. I wonder, do they realize our for-profit medical system is run by an oil man? What does that tell you? If you have a hammer, everything is a nail. So, if you have oil and find out that it is sweet and addictive, you plan to only use it as a band aid to make people feel good, while the root of the problem is never addressed. So no cures. See the whole idea is to keep people tied to our for-profit medical system. It appears this band aid method is used in everything from pain pills to anxiety pills. No wonder people find they get addicted to them. And that it is hell when they try to wean themselves off of them.

Evidently, the general public does not see this. I guess that is why being a starseed from Alcyone of the Pleiades I am here to help. So I am here to do the investigating and the research. I am here to read, look and listen and take note, and report back to the Pleiadians who are also members of the Galactic Federation. Of course, the Galactic Federation sees what is going on, they don't have spacecrafts encircling Earth for nothing. Their spacecrafts are just hovering nearby waiting to be summoned. They wish to help humans try to save themselves and the planet from the evil reptiles that lurk beneath our feet hiding in caves below the Earth. You know the evil reptilian humanoid hybrid males that try to pretend to be human someday will have to answer to their supreme ruling reptiles that hide underground. The evil ones running the works, are mere shape-shifting reptilian humanoid hybrids posing as human beings. Of course, without a soul or conscience, they have no moral compass, no soul decency to guide them. They only know threats of death by toxins in their aim to destroy all living things on planet Earth that are organic, and that, I am sorry to say, appears to include you.

I am here working with my guides and my Pleiadian family to attempt to awaken and enlighten the populations. There is no hierarchy or competition as we Pleiadians work together for the greater good of all. So it is why I read and try to learn how we can keep ourselves healthy, and to use mind over matter. J.Z. Knight who channels the spirit Ramtha says, "We can reverse conditions and heal ourselves, even grow younger in mind, body and spirit."

There are simple things we can do to improve our health like walking barefoot, or using a grounding sheet, or mattress cover to sleep on every night. I haven't missed a night in over three years. And I feel great! Also help yourself by making sure you buy and eat organic foods. I see people drinking regular Pepsi made with High Fructose Corn Syrup or Drinking Diet Pepsi made with Aspartame. Don't you get the feeling that they are trying to make us all sick? Are they all in cahoots to make us sick to keep us going back to the doctor. Yes, the audacity, that the government permits toxic chemicals to go in food and drinks. I feel we, the people, we taxpayers, have no government protection whatsoever. We the people have to beg for everything, while the corporations buy their favors. I feel these reptilian humanoid hybrids in high government and corporate positions will be the ruin of us yet, unless the Galactic Federation steps in and either tweets the moon's computer, or shuts it down all together. They say the moon controls the seasons and the high and low tides. If they shut it down, I believe we will know, for there will be no high or low tide, who knows maybe women will even stop having their monthly periods.

I have to remind myself that I am indeed a starseed from Alcyone of the Pleiades, as I have empathy. And I do know better. I should not take in their emotional states or their physical symptoms like the misery loves company syndrome. So, it appears to me that the evil powers just might want us ill and injured from side effects to keep people coming back for more.

So might I suggest everyone who had the c19 jabs, use nicotine patches or gummies, take Melatonin, and eat foods that contain nicotine such as cabbage, pineapple, potatoes, black pepper, cayenne pepper, and all colors of bell peppers. Raisins and plums also contain nicotine.

If left alone to live as organic beings which we are, I believe we would grow stronger with age, like a tree. This country and now the world has been invaded by evil soulless reptiles and their puppets that look and try to act like they have human emotions, but they just can't quit pull it off.

I believe as time goes on, and more evidence is exposed, we the people are catching on, and the Galactic Federation as I write this is reining in on their evil ways and toning them down before the whole of Earth becomes one prison planet. Sometimes, I feel I am about the only one that actually sees what is happening. I believe getting the word out with this book and *DianneTheMedium* podcast at PodBean is what I am called to do.

I have gotten hints along the way. The first, Rosie my guide told me I am the medium, she will bring only the good spirits forward. After that miraculous event, the Pleiadians told me in that classroom, with the two witnesses, that I was from Alcyone, the brightest and central star of the Pleiades. And I believe they set it up for me to attend the seminar by Mavis Pittalla, the grand dame of Mediumship from England. It was a wonderful experience and I thank my Pleiadian guides for letting me know about it. I learned a lot. Mavis Pittalla had me give a random speech on the spur of the moment.

"Your word is courage," Mavis said.

I had to think fast, as I was standing in front of a classroom of sixty-four souls waiting for me to speak. I quickly recalled hints from high school speech class.

Look around the room, and speak clearly and say the words often. I know my Pleiadians guides helped me. Because when I looked out over the classroom I saw only smiling faces, eager to hear what I had to say. When I was finished, Mavis and her partner Jane, both said I should be a writer, a speaker, perhaps a life coach. My wonderful guides and the Pleiadians seem to have always been with me as I grew up and all through my adult life. I am most grateful to be on the spiritual path they have led me on.

Chapter Twenty-Three:

Pleiadians Paving The Way

I believe my Pleiadian guides really have been with me since I was a small child. I was healthy. I am a Libra. I have a lot of "air" in my Astrology natal birth chart, and my sun was in the twelve houses of spiritual connection. Lots of Air in my Astrological natal birth chart means spiritual, psychic and intuitive. I think the Pleiadian energy really kicked in when my dad beat our German Shepard to death, and I felt that I was next in line to be killed. That was when I felt I had no allies. But then I saw a vision of a spiritual being then, a woman with blonde curly hair, and she wore glasses. I no longer felt alone as I knew she was one of my guides there to comfort me.

My guides helped me all through my school years, and had my mother become a beautician, so that I would be a beautician too when I was still in High School. I worked as a beautician part-time when I went to work full-time at a bank. While working there, my friend who worked for SouthWestern Bell Telephone

(SWBT) told me three times that SWBT was hiring clerks and I applied. I did not listen at first, but I got hired there as a clerk. What really convinced me was I was out one evening at our regular lounge, and a guy came along and asked each one of us standing in a group, where did we worked. My friend Nancy said, "Ralston Purina." He said, "Oh that is a good job." Carol P said she worked at Laclede Gas. "Oh that is a good job," he said. My other friend Carol H who worked at SWBT phone company said where she worked. "Oh that is a good job." Then he asked me where I worked and I said at the First National Bank and he said, "Banks do not pay very well, do they?"

Boy, that did it for me. I immediately applied at the phone company. See how my Pleiadians guides sent that guy to ask us where we worked? That is how spirit works. They do have their ways. So I was hired on as a clerk. When Affirmative Action came to be, I put my transfer in for a technician craft job.

A few weeks later, the union steward informed me I was passed up, so I would be offered the next technician craft job. When I learned what the first job involved, I was glad that I was passed up, because I would have taken it. It was an outside pole-climbing job, which would have meant, working in all kinds of weather, and putting up with weeds, poison ivy, bees, wasps, and snakes in technical equipment boxes. So I thanked my guides and the Pleiadians that I was passed up.

The next job that came along and I accepted. It was perfect. It was an inside control center job monitoring a bank of computers, trouble shooting, editing programming code, and loading the software. It was a twenty-four-hour, seven day a week job. I was low in seniority. One day my boss came to me and asked for my help.

"Dianne, I need to cover two people's days off," he stated, "maybe you can help me out." He needed to cover the four to midnight two days off and he needed to cover the midnight to eight in the morning shift.

"I have an idea," I said, "why don't I work to midnight on Friday and Saturday, stay, then and work midnight to eight on Sunday, Monday and Tuesday." So I only had to drive to work four times, and got to park in the garage since I was not working day-time hours.

"You would do that?" he asked.

"Sure," was my reply. Actually, I loved it. Because then I had from eight in the morning on Tuesday until Friday afternoon at four off. I was low on seniority and had to work every holiday. I did this for nine years until some guy bumped me off that tour. So I thanked my guides every day for that golden opportunity. And later on when that center moved to Dallas, I was considered surplus. That was when I was seeing Jeannine the psychic medium who channeled Ezekiel. And he told me that my job would move away, but I would get a job in the adjacent building.

And that came true. I got to stay in St. Louis. My next job was in Special Services in the installation division, where I trouble-shot new circuits, and tested them end to end before the installer got to the customer site.

Installing circuits for bank ATM machines would be an example. I loved the job, as I loved trouble shooting. Thank you, my guides and Pleiadians. A few years later when that job was moved to Dallas, I had the age and service number of years where I could accept the buyout and retire. Thank you, my guides and Pleiadians.

Getting that first position and working those off hours made it easy for me to save up enough money for a down payment on a condo. See, while I worked that clerk clerical job. I could never get ahead enough to save up a down payment. But, by getting a "man's" salary when I got the technology craft job, I could easily save the money for the down payment. I was finally able to quickly save enough money for a down payment, or I never would have been able to buy my first condo with woman's job clerk's pay. Get it? Another thing my wonderful guides did for me: guide me to good savings.

Since I worked for the phone company, I dealt with the Telephone Credit Union. When I was still a clerk during the President Carter years, inflation and interest rates were high on loans and on savings accounts. So I went to the credit union and said I wanted to put my money into a Certificate of Deposit they were offering. She said the interest rate is 18%, or was it 23%? Anyway, I locked it in for the full three years that was offered. Years later I was talking to a guy who had worked for the phone company credit union. He admitted it was people like me who locked that Certificate of Deposit in for three years at that high interest rate who nearly ruined the credit union. Because after I locked that high earnings interest rate in, the market rate when down, and the interest rates went down, even for loans. So the credit union had trouble recouping, making enough money from loans, to pay for investors like me who locked in for three years interest on their Certificates of Deposit. So my guides helped me and I lucked out again, and in the end the credit union did too the guy said.

So when I was a clerk at the phone company, along came Affirmative Action, and all I have to do was put my transfer in to get a higher paying craft job, in other words god forbid, a man's job. The union steward told me that I was passed on the first offer and said I would get the next offer. I came to realize that getting passed up on the first offer, was a gift from my Pleiadian guides, as it was an outside job that required climbing poles. And the one I was offered was to be an inside job, and when I heard the description of it, I knew I was well suited for it. As it was a position in the Packet Switch control center monitoring a bank of computer monitors and initiating and working on installation and then trouble shooting trouble tickets. I came to love trouble shooting.

And when my job moved to Texas in the mid-1990s I was then seeing Jeannine the psychic medium who channeled Ezekiel, and he told me I would not have to move away but would move to the adjacent building. And that is exactly what happened. As the Packet Switch center moved to Dallas, I moved into the next adjacent building and got a job in Special Services installation crew, as a new circuit tester, I loved trouble shooting. My job was to make sure the circuit was tested end to end between the long distance carrier company and the end customer, where the installer would be installing the high capacity circuits. So, I did not have to move to Texas, thank you my Pleiadian guides.

Also right around that time, 1995 to be exact, my wonderful guides were with me via my best friend as we worked together. I was lucky enough to have her be scheduled to go to a company school with me in Texas. The 1995 class in Dallas, at the company school, was a pass-fail class. Fail you were out of there, out of the company, I mean. I had failed the first round, and you got two tries. I was nervous as my job depended on my passing the class. My wonderful guides and the Pleiadians, neither of them I had met yet because I met the Pleiadians in 2015, and Rosie my guide in 2016, were there. My good friend had her class on the same subject a day ahead of mine. I think my good boss, who created that great five-day work tour for me, in appreciation arranged it so my good friend would travel with me, but her class started on a Monday and mine on a Tuesday. See, he knew that I had to pass it or lose my job. So, he arranged for her class to start the day before mine, and she could help me by studying with me to prepare for my tests. It was perfect; she could help me know the answers for my class for the next day. Perfect. She even had a Valium for me when I needed it in my pass-fail required, or lose your job tests. Oh Yes! Nervous times! You see, I failed the first round of the class, and you get two tries at it. So everything weighed heavy on this round. But I passed, thanks to my considerate boss, my best friend, and my wonderful Pleiadian guides.

A few years later around 2003 when the second wave of moving the business to the Dallas Headquarters was conducted, I just so happened to be the right age, and have the right amount of service years, to accept the buyout and retire. Thank you, my guides. So now you see why I feel blessed and honored to be a starseed from Alcyone of the Pleiades.

And may I suggest to everyone reading this, they get to know your spiritual guides. While you are doing that, take a moment to look back on your life, and see if you can connect the dots to see those magical moments where your guides have helped you. Because even though you have not yet met them, like I have, they are there with you, so you can thank them anyway.

Chapter Twenty-Four:

Know Your Guide Hints

These are special times and good times to get to know your guides. Also read and watch GAIA interviews, especially Open Minds with Regina Meredith as she has many different psychic medium guests on her series of episodes. Many channel and have spirit speak through them. My Pleiadian and other guides speak through me, telepathically, and out loud using my voice on my *DianneTheMedium* podcast at PodBean. And they help guide me through my research reading for the podcast and for writing my books. My Pleiadian guides also gave me the gift to see the big picture and not be mind-controlled by the negative frequencies of the reptilian programmed Moon computer, television commercials, the bought-up and brought-to-you by corporate talking head news, especially cable news, or through, mind-controlled or trained which ever word you prefer, programmed doctors and other medical personal. It is shocking and appalling to me, as I am sure it is to all other awakened and enlightened people on Earth. Is this America? Land of the free? How is it that I had to come the reality and face the horrendous truth. As actions certainly speak louder than words, it is becoming obvious to me and many other people and I hate to have to say it. We have been under attack by the greed and corruption that are in power. And what is most alarming is that we apparently have no protection against it.

Humans are like sitting ducks surrounded by baby flesh eaters of the underground reptiles. We must be living under a Moon produced hologram of science fiction. I refuse to believe otherwise. The Galactic Federation is our only hope for planet survival at this point. My Pleiadian guides have enlightened me to realize that allopathic medicine is not working, and more people are going full circle and leaning toward holistic medicine. Only we can heal ourselves through our healthy immune systems, it's why we need organic foods.

I am most grateful to my Pleiadians guides encouraging me on when I write my books. For example, when I wrote, "Pleasant View," I got the idea while I was talking to my friend one day. She was telling me that her neighbor was selling her condo and moving into a retirement center. She said a very nice one where they take care of everything for you, even investing your life savings for you.

"And they cook for them too," I asked.

"Yes of course."

That gave me the idea for the book. So I set the book in

the 1980's where this wanting to get rich quick, woman and her husband own a retirement center. She is looking for an unsavory cook to do her bidding. I needed a poison for the cook to use. So I went to the library to get ideas. While reading the *USA Today*, I came upon an article of a story of a man who went mushroom hunting in California. He found so many he wanted to share them with the local senior retirement home, yes the exact scenario. Bad idea, since the mushrooms turned out to be toxic. The article even gave the technical name for the mushrooms. So I adapted a version of that story to use for my book. So I thanked my Pleiadian guides for helping me.

Also, I think my Pleiadians guides wanted me to write my book entitled, *Verda*. *Verda* is all about evil sneaky reptiles running a planet call Verda. And the reptiles are hiding underground, but they have their reptilian humanoid hybrid slaves that have scratched and clawed their way to powerful positions of government and corporate boardroom. Sound familiar? Their secret mission is to depopulate the planet. So, they came up with a fake virus, and persuaded people via the media that in order to save lives they must get the injection. To make sure people get the jab, they get the government to mandate government employees to get it. They use fear tactics and say that everyone must get the inoculations to prevent getting the claimed deadly virus. Turns out my Pleiadian mind-set was correct sorry to say, as side effects indicated that the kill was in the fix, not the fake virus as most people got the virus after they got the jab. I know that the Pleiadians helped guide me with writing that book.

I appreciate their guidance and good will, keeping me, as the saying goes, healthy, wealthy and wise and trying to help others awaken, and raise their vibrations up to the fifth dimension of Aquarian feminine rule. I believe it is way the Pleiadians led me to read certain books and then encouraged me to create *DianneTheMedium* podcast on PodBean to do the work of the Pleiades.

I am most grateful my Pleiadian guides gave me the opportunity to learn I am from Alcyone of the Pleiades and I wish to honor that privilege and present them well by writing this book and by doing my podcast on *DianneTheMedium* at PodBean. Also by offering free mediumship readings on zoom. Just go to my contact page at DianneTheMedium.com and send me an email. Might I suggest that we all get to know our guides by raising your vibrations doing acts of kindness, meditating, getting out into nature.

I believe that my guides led me to learning about grounding. Either by walking barefoot in the grass to going to earthing.com and buying an Earthing mattress cover that plugs into the grounding port on an electrical outlet. When you order from them, they send along a book of healthy testimonies. All I know is that it works. I do not think that I have missed sleeping on a grounding mattress cover, or smaller travel side 12x36 inch grounding pad I use when I travel, since I bought it at least three years ago. And I do believe that it makes a difference as I feel very well, have lost weight and have more energy. I even got a pad for the seat of my car. The pad has a cord and an alligator clip that clipped on to the medal part on the seat frame.

Might I suggest everyone watch the Grounding documentary on Netflix. I recently received the book The Mother Earth Effect Connect to the Earth and Heal by Elisabeth Hoekstra and Olivia Ramirez Smith with foreword by Clinton Ober. It is a 117-page book filled with the testimonies from people who had physical problems and by sleeping grounded have found relief from swelling, pain, and noticed stress reduction. The ground specialist suggests getting out in the sun, and walking barefoot in the grass. I have slept grounded every night uninterrupted for at least three years now, ever since I discovered Clinton Ober's documentary on Netflix. I believe my Pleiadian guides had me see that documentary and persuaded me to order a mattress cover, and it was around Christmas time when earthing. com had their fifty percent off original price sale. See how the Pleiadians guide me, not only to books, housing, and social groups but to learning about grounding, good nutrition and good healthy supplements to ward off illness, and to go organic and holistic health care if needed. So, meditate get out in nature, and get to know your guides. And read books by David Icke.

Chapter Twenty Four:

Taurus Sun

I was looking through *Everything You Need to Know but Have Never Been Told* by David Icke and I came across his birthday information of date, place, but not time. So I decided to use my current time for when I saw his birth information, because I figured my Pleiadian guides helped me find his birthday information and had me pick up his book and look through it at this particular time of the day for a reason. I choose his birth time at 1:30 p.m. Mountain time as I am in Arizona at the moment I write this. His birthday is April 29, 1952, Leicester, England I used 1:30 p.m.

I am not surprised that his sun is in the sign of Taurus. So he is from the Pleiades, so David Icke is a Pleiadian. Amazing isn't it. No wonder I was drawn to his books. And at 1:30 p.m. his sun, conjunct with Jupiter are in the sign of Taurus (anything in Taurus means you are from the Pleiades) and in the ninth house of Sagittarius (Sagittarius ruled by Jupiter and also Jupiter rules over laws and social order and the ninth house) So he not only has his Taurus sun influence, he has the ninth house influence of adventure, sports, travel, and freedom and speaks with a blunt tongue. Key word for ninth house is "idealize." The sign of Taurus mean "possess" and can be stubborn in their quest for truths and healing and being an earth sign, they can endure. Reading his books, I see where in 1992, I believe it was, he was contacted by an other worldly source and directed to the book Mind to Mind by Betty Shine. He read her book in a day and then made an appointment to visit Betty Shine. It's amazing the books he has written since then.

I should have figured that David Icke would be a Pleiadian. Any planet, asteroid, Sun, Moon, south or north node of the Moon in the sign of Taurus means that you are from the Pleiades, and are a Pleiadian. David Icke has his Sun in Taurus, conjunct Jupiter, the planet of expansion. So he is really wholehearted into his mission of revealing the truths, as his many books have demonstrated. So looking at this Astrological natal chart makes me firmly believe that he is indeed a Pleiadian on a mission trying to enrich and enlighten mankind and to help lift humankind up into the higher vibrations of the fifth dimension, and to overcome the evils that have been placed on humankind by the evil reptilian humanoid hybrid illuminati slaves puppets which are manipulated by the evil reptiles still hiding and living underground.

According to what I have read, now the reptiles wish to expose themselves and walk amongst the humans in their original form and no longer shape-shifting appearing as reptilian humanoid hybrids but in there full reptilian form. And I do believe that this will happen if and when Agenda 2030 comes to be, and no one or group rises up to stop him. I believe the Galactic Federation can only fly their spacecraft around Washington D.C. like they did in 1952 (there is video footage) and again in 1953, which never made the news. If the evil ones have their way all of planet Earth. Toxic pills and jabs have always been an attack on the human immune system.

Read the book *The Poisoned Needle Suppressed Facts about Vaccination* by Eleanor McBean written in 1957. See, they knew way back then, that vaccinations did not have any benefits. Also read *The Medical Voodoo* by Annie Riley Hale a book about mad scientist written in 1935. Also may I suggest the book by Dr. John Yiamouylannis written first edition, published in 1983. So my mission, at this time at the end of 2023, is to do my best to enlighten and awaken people to raise their vibrations to the fifth dimension of the Age of Aquarius of feminine rule of the new world. And isn't it about time that Earth becomes a little more like the Pleiades in the respect of females once again cleaning up the messes these few evil males have created out of ruthless, without a soul consciousness, greed.

To learn more visit *DianneTheMedium* podcast at PodBean and visit my DianneTheMedium.com website for a free mediumship reading. Just go to my contact page and send me a request for a free zoom mediumship reading (it works just as well using zoom). I will get back with you and we can decide on a day and time for your free reading. I usually suggest that you set aside at least an hour for the reading.

The way I understand it is that the Galactic Federation is overseeing what is going on, but cannot interfere unless summoned. People are indeed waking up to the corruption that surrounds us. People are learning to go holistic and organic and learning to keep themselves well. People are learning that grounding is very beneficial for all that ails the human body and mind. Vitamins and minerals are what humans need to build up their internal pharmacy, which is their immune system. All things to ponder as we begin the year 2024. Whatever happens, I know that my guides Rosie, Emma, Steve and the Pleiadians will be guiding me.

About the Author

This is Dianne Zimmermann's ninth book, and her first non-fictional book. Dianne shares her time between St. Louis and Sedona. She is an Alcyone Pleiadian starseed and a psychic medium. Dianne enjoys writing, painting, drawing, biking, hiking, and road trips. She also enjoys performing at open mic events as "DianneZ and her Ukulele," a lounge singer. She croons the old standard favorites in her unique singing and ukulele strumming style.

She can be contacted at DianneTheMedium.com for free zoom mediumship readings and singing engagements. Listen to *DianneTheMedium* podcast at PodBean.

www.ingramcontent.com/pod-product-compliance
Lightning Source LLC
Chambersburg PA
CBHW031515120626
46545CB00005B/1894